First German Reader for Students

Steven Reed

First German Reader for Students
Bilingual for Speakers of English
Level A1 and A2

First German Reader for Students

by Steven Reed

Series Title: Graded German Readers, Volume 10

Audio tracks www.lppbooks.com/German/FGRS/

Homepage www.audiolego.com

Design: Audiolego Design

Images: Canstockphoto

First edition

Copyright © 2016 Language Practice Publishing

Copyright © 2016 Audiolego

This book is in copyright. Subject to statutory exception and to the provisions of relevant collective licensing agreements, no reproduction of any part may take place without the written permission of Language Practice Publishing.

Inhaltsverzeichnis
Table of contents

How to control the playing speed 7
Das deutsche Alphabet 8
Kapitel 1 Die Küche 11
Kapitel 2 Wo ist das Speisezimmer? 18
Kapitel 3 Der Saal 23
Kapitel 4 Das Badezimmer 27
Kapitel 5 Kannst du Deutsch oder Spanisch sprechen? 31
Kapitel 6 Kannst du mir helfen? 36
Kapitel 7 Wie heißt du? 42
Kapitel 8 Der Weg zur Universität 49
Kapitel 9 Ich gehe gerne ins Kino 54
Kapitel 10 Jack will Rechtsanwalt werden 60
Kapitel 11 Jack ist krank 69
Kapitel 12 Jack will eine neue Wohnung finden 75
Kapitel 13 Im Geschäft 84
Kapitel 14 Heute habe ich vier Fächer 91
Kapitel 15 Jack will eine Teilzeitarbeit finden 100
Wörterbuch Deutsch-Englisch 106
Wörterbuch Englisch-Deutsch 119
Starke Verben 132
Wichtige Adjektive 138
Körperliche Eigenschaften 139
Gegenteile 140
List of the most common words 141
Days of the week 141
Months 141
Seasons of the year 141
Family 141
Appearance and qualities 142
Emotions 142
Clothes 143
House and furniture 143
Kitchen 144

Tableware	145
Food	145
Meat and fish	146
Fruit	147
Vegetables	147
Beverages	147
Cooking	148
Housekeeping	148
Body care	148
Weather	149
Transport	149
City	150
School	151
Professions	152
Actions	153
Music	154
Sports	155
Body	155
Nature	156
Pet	157
Animals	157
Birds	158
Flowers	158
Trees	158
Sea	159
Colors	159
Size	160
Materials	160
Airport	160
Geography	161
Crimes	162
Numbers	162
Ordinal numbers	163
Recommended reading	164

How to control the playing speed

The book is equipped with the audio tracks. The address of the home page of the book on the Internet, where audio files are available for listening and downloading, is listed at the beginning of the book on the bibliographic description page before the copyright notice.

We recommend using free **VLC media player** to control the playing speed. You can control the playing speed by decreasing or increasing the speed value on the button of the VLC media player's interface.

Android users: After installing VLC media player, click an audio track at the top of a chapter or on the home page of the book if you read a paper book. When prompted choose "Open with VLC". If you experience difficulties opening audio tracks with VLC, change default app for music player. Go to Settings→Apps, choose VLC and click "Open by default" or "Set default".

Kindle Fire users: After installing VLC media player, click an audio track at the top of a chapter or on the home page of the book if you read a paper book. Complete action using →VLC.

iOS users: After installing VLC media player, copy the link to an audio track at the top of a chapter or on the home page of the book if you read a paper book. Paste it into Downloads section of VLC media player. After the download is complete, go to All Files section and start the downloaded audio track.

Windows users: After installing VLC media player, right-click an audio track at the top of a chapter or on the home page of the book if you read a paper book. Choose "Open with→VLC media player".

MacOS users: After installing VLC media player, right-click an audio track at the top of a chapter or on the home page of the book if you read a paper book, then download it. Right-click the downloaded audio track and choose "Get info". Then in the "Open with" section choose VLC media player. You can enable "Change all" to apply this change to all audio tracks.

Das deutsche Alphabet

The German alphabet

Buchstabe Letter	Handschrift Handwriting	Aussprache Pronunciation	Beispiele Examples
A a	A a	ah	Apfel (apple)
Ä ä	Ä ä	ay	Äpfel (apples)
B b	B b	bay	Buch (book)
C c	C c	say	Café
D d	D d	day	Doch (however)
E e	E e	ay	Rede (speach)
F f	F f	eff	Fahren (go, drive)
G g	G g	gay	Gast (guest)
H h	H h	haa	Hoch (high)
I i	I i	eeh	Lippe (lip)
J j	J j	yot	Ja (yes)
K k	K k	kah	Kuss (kiss, *n*)
L l	L l	ell	Leben (live)

M m	M m	emm	Mutter (mother)
N n	N n	enn	Nord (north)
O o	O o	oh	Ort (place, *n*)
Ö ö	Ö ö	oeh	Öl (oil)
P p	P p	pay	Preis (price)
Q q	Q q	koo	Quadrat (square)
R r	R r	err	Rose (rose)
S s	S s	ess	Sofa (sofa)
ß	ß	ess-zett (s-z ligature)	Straße (street), *lower case only, replaces "ss" in some words.*
T t	T t	tay	Tag (day)
U u	U u	ueh	unter (below)
Ü ü	Ü ü	uyuh	über (over, about)
V v	V v	fow	vier (four)
W w	W w	vay	Woche (week)
X x	X x	ixx	Xylofon

Y y	Y y	oop-see-lohn	Typ (type)
Z z	Z z	zett	zu (to)

Diphthongs

Diphthong Double Vowels	Aussprache Pronunciation	Beispiele / Examples
ai / ei	eye	Ein (one), Mai (May)
au	ow	auch (also)
eu / äu	oy	Häuser (houses), neu (new)
ie	eeh	Sie (you), nie (never)

Grouped Consonants

Buchstabe Consonant	Aussprache Pronunciation	Beispiele / Examples
ck	k	Glük (happyness)
ch	kh	Auch (too), sounds like "sh" or like "kh"
pf	pf	Pfeil (arrow)
ph	f	Alphabet (alphabet)
qu	kv	Quark (curd)
sch	sh	Schule (school)
sp / st	shp / sht	Sprechen (speak), Straße (street) at the beginning of a stem only, otherwise sp/st
th	t	Theater (theatre), never pronounced like the English th

1

Die Küche

The kitchen

A

Vokabeln

1. alt - old
2. auch - also, too
3. auf - on
4. aus, von - from, out of
5. Ausguss, der; das Becken - sink
6. bequem - comfortable
7. Bild, das - picture
8. Blender, der - blender
9. Blume, die - flower
10. Dach, das - roof
11. das - this
12. Decke, die - ceiling
13. Ecke, die - corner
14. eingehen - to go into

15. er/sie/es - he/she/it
16. es gibt, es sind - there is, there are
17. Fenster, das - window
18. Fisch, der - fish
19. Flur, der - hall
20. für - for
21. Gabel, die - fork
22. Garten, der - garden
23. Gas- - gas (adj.)
24. gegenüber - across from
25. gelb - yellow
26. gemütlich - cozy, comfortable
27. geräumig - spacious
28. Geschirr, das - dishes
29. Glas, das - glass
30. Glas-, gläsern - glass (adj.)
31. grau - gray
32. Griff, der - handle
33. groß - big
34. grün - green
35. Gummi- - rubber (adj.)
36. hängen - to hang
37. Haus, das - house
38. Herd, der - stove
39. hinter - behind, for
40. hölzern, Holz- - wooden
41. Hühnchen, das - chicken
42. Hund, der - dog
43. in - in
44. ja - yes

45. Kaffeemaschine, die - coffeemaker
46. Katze, die - cat
47. klein - small
48. Kronleuchter, der - chandelier
49. Küche, die - kitchen
50. Küchen- - kitchen (adj.)
51. Kühlschrank, der - refrigerator
52. laufen - to run
53. leicht - light (adj.)
54. links - on the left
55. Löffel, der - spoon
56. metallen, Metall- - metal (adj.)
57. mit - with
58. Mixer, der - mixer
59. nah, in der Nähe - near
60. nein; es gibt kein(e/en) - no; there isn't, there aren't
61. neu - new
62. ober - on top of, over, above
63. oder - or
64. rechts - on the right
65. rot - red
66. rund - round
67. sauber - clean
68. Schiff, das - ship
69. schmutzig - dirty
70. schön - pretty, beautiful
71. Schrank, der; das Regal - cupboard, wardrobe, bookcase
72. See, die; das Meer - sea
73. Serviette, die - napkin

74. sich befinden - to be (located)
75. sorgfältig - careful
76. Stadt, die - city
77. stehen - to stand
78. stehlen - to steal
79. Straße, die - street
80. Stuhl, der - chair
81. Tasse, die - cup
82. Tee- - tea (adj.)
83. Teekessel, der - teapot
84. Teller, der - plate
85. Tisch, der - table
86. Tischtuch, das - tablecloth
87. Toaster, der - toaster
88. treten, trampeln - to trample
89. trinken - to drink
90. Trockner, der; der Fön (für die Haare) - drier
91. Tür, die - door
92. und - and
93. Wand, die - wall
94. was - what
95. Waschen, das - washer, washing
96. Wasser, das - water
97. weiß - white
98. wir - we
99. wo - where
100. wollen - to want
101. zu Hause - at home

B

Das ist eine Stadt. Sie ist groß und schön. Sie liegt in der Nähe der See.

Das ist eine Straße. Sie liegt in der Stadt. Die Straße ist groß und sauber.

Das ist ein Haus. Das Haus liegt an der Straße. Es ist angenehm und schön. Die Wände sind weiß. Das Dach ist rot. Die Tür ist neu. Sie ist aus Holz.

Das ist ein Garten. Der Garten liegt an dem Haus. Er ist groß und grün. Ein Hund verfolgt ein Hühnchen im Garten. Er trampelt über die Blumen.

Wir gehen ins Haus ein. Das ist der Flur. Der Flur ist geräumig und bequem.

This is a city. It is big and beautiful. It is located near the sea.

This is a street. It is in the city. The street is large and clean.

This is a house. The house is in the street. It is neat and beautiful. The walls are white. The roof is red. The door is new. It is wooden.

This is a garden. The garden is located near the house. It's big and green. A dog is running after a chicken in the garden. It tramples on flowers.

We go into the house. This is a hall. The hall is spacious and comfortable.

Rechts ist die Küche. Die Küche ist groß und hell. Die Wände sind gelb. Die Decke ist weiß.

Es gibt einen Kronleuchter unter der Decke. Er ist groß und schön.

Das ist ein Tisch. Er ist groß und rund. Ein Tischtuch liegt auf dem Tisch.

Das ist ein Mixer. Er liegt auf dem Tisch. Er ist bequem und klein.

Das ist ein Glas. Es steht auch auf dem Tisch. Es ist gläsern. Das Glas ist sauber.

Neben dem Tisch steht ein Stuhl. Er ist aus Holz. Der Stuhl ist bequem.

Das ist ein Kühlschrank. Er ist grau. Der Kühlschrank ist neu. Er steht in der Ecke. Eine Katze sitzt neben dem Kühlschrank. Sie will aus dem Kühlschrank einen Fisch stehlen.

Das ist ein Toaster. Er steht auf dem Kühlschrank. Er ist klein und praktisch.

Das ist eine Kaffeemaschine. Sie steht neben dem Ausguss. Die Kaffeemaschine ist schmutzig.

Das ist ein Blender. Er steht auch auf dem Kühlschrank. Er ist weiß. Der Blender ist alt.

Gegenüber des Kühlschranks gibt es ein Fenster. Es ist groß und sauber.

Das ist ein Herd. Er befindet sich neben dem Fenster. Er ist neu und praktisch.

Das ist ein Teekessel. Es steht auf dem Gasherd. Es ist metallen und hat einen Griff aus Gummi.

Neben dem Kühlschrank steht eine Spülmaschine. Links gibt es einen Trockner für das Geschirr.

Das ist ein Regal. Er hängt über dem Ausguss. Er ist aus Holz.

The kitchen is on the right. The kitchen is large and bright. The walls are yellow. The ceiling is white.

There is a chandelier on the ceiling. It is big and beautiful.

This is a table. It's big and round. There is a tablecloth on the table.

This is a mixer. It is on the table. It's comfortable and small.

This is a glass. It is also on the table. It is made of glass. The glass is clean.

Near the table there is a chair. It is wooden. The chair is comfortable.

This is a refrigerator. It is gray. The refrigerator is new. It is located in the corner. There is a cat near the refrigerator. He wants to steal fish from the refrigerator.

This is a toaster. It is standing on the refrigerator. The toaster is small and convenient.

This is a coffee maker. It is standing near the sink. The coffee maker is dirty.

This is a blender. It is also on the refrigerator. It is white. The blender is old.

Across from the refrigerator, there is a window. It is large and clean.

This is a stove. It is located near the window. It is new and convenient

This is a kettle. It is on a gas stove. It is metal with a rubber handle.

Near the refrigerator there is a dishwasher. To the left, there is a dryer for dishes.

This is a cupboard. It hangs over the

Das ist eine Serviette. Es liegt in dem Küchenregal. Es ist klein und sauber.

Das ist ein Bild. Es hängt auf der Wand. Es gibt das Meer und ein Schiff auf dem Bild.

Das ist der Küchentisch. Er steht in der Ecke. Er ist groß und hölzern.

Das ist eine Gabel. Sie liegt auf dem Küchentisch. Die Gabel ist aus Metall. Sie ist klein.

Das ist ein Teller. Er steht auf dem Küchentisch. Der Teller ist gelb. Er ist klein und schön.

Das ist eine Tasse. Sie steht auch auf dem Küchentisch. Die Tasse ist rot. Eine Katze trinkt Wasser aus der Tasse.

Das ist ein Teelöffel. Er befindet sich in einer Tasse. Der Löffel ist aus Metall. Er ist klein.

sink. It is wooden.

This is a napkin. It is in the kitchen cupboard. It's small and clean.

This is a picture. It is on the wall. There is the sea and a ship in the painting.

This is the kitchen table. It is located in the corner. It is large and wooden.

This is a fork. It is on the kitchen table. The fork is metal. It is small.

This is a dish. It is on the kitchen table. The plate is yellow. It's small and beautiful.

This is a cup. It is also on the kitchen table. The cup is red. A cat drinks water from the cup.

This is a teaspoon. It is located in a cup. The spoon is metal. It's small.

C

Fragen und Antworten

- Wo ist die Stadt?
- Sie liegt in der Nähe der See.
- Ist die Straße groß oder klein?
- Die Straße ist groß.
- Wo ist das Haus?
- Das Haus ist in der Straße.
- Wo ist der Garten?
- Der Garten befindet sich neben dem Haus.
- Ist der Garten groß oder klein?
- Der Garten ist groß.

Questions and Answers

- Where is the city?
- It is located near the sea.
- Is the street big or small?
- The street is big.
- Where is the house?
- The house is in the street.
- Where is the garden?
- The garden is located near the house.
- The garden is large or small?
- The garden is large.

- Ist der Flur geräumig?
- Ja, der Flur ist geräumig.
- Wo ist die Küche?
- Die Küche ist rechts.
- Wo ist der Mixer?
- Der Mixer liegt auf dem Tisch.
- Gibt es ein Tischtuch auf dem Tisch?
- Ja, es gibt ein Tischtuch auf dem Tisch.
- Was gibt es auf dem Tisch?
- Es gibt ein Glas auf dem Tisch.
- Ist das Glas schmutzig?
- Nein, das Glas ist sauber.
- Wo ist der Kühlschrank?
- Der Kühlschrank steht in der Ecke.
- Wo ist die Katze?
- Die Katze sitzt neben dem Kühlschrank.
- Wo ist die Kaffeemaschine?
- Die Kaffeemaschine ist neben dem Ausguss.
- Ist die Kaffeemaschine sauber?
- Nein, sie ist schmutzig.
- Gibt es ein Fenster in der Küche?
- Ja, das Fenster ist neben dem Kühlschrank.
- Ist das Fenster groß?
- Ja, es ist groß.
- Wo ist die Gabel?
- Sie liegt auf dem Küchentisch.
- Ist der Teller auch auf dem Küchentisch?
- Ja, es gibt auch einen Teller auf dem Küchentisch.
- Gibt es Servietten in der Küche?

- Is the hall spacious?
- Yes, the hall is spacious.
- Where's the kitchen?
- Kitchen is on the right.
- Where is the mixer?
- The mixer on the table.
- Is there a tablecloth on the table?
- Yes, there is a tablecloth on the table.
- What is there on the table?
- There is a glass on the table.
- It is dirty?
- No, the glass is clean.
- Where's the fridge?
- The refrigerator is in the corner.
- Where is the cat?
- The cat is near the refrigerator.
- Where is coffeemaker?
- The coffeemaker is near the sink.
- Is the coffeemaker clean?
- No, it's dirty.
- Is there a window in the kitchen?
- Yes, the window is near the refrigerator.
- Is the window large?
- Yes, it's large.
- Where is the fork?
- The fork is on the kitchen table.
- Is the plate also on the kitchen table?
- Yes, a plate is on the kitchen table.
- Are there napkins in the kitchen?

- Ja, es gibt Servietten in dem Küchenregal.
- Gibt eine saubere Tasse in der Küche?
- Ja, es gibt eine saubere Tasse in der Küche.
- Ist die Tasse rot?
- Ja, sie ist rot.

- Yes, there are napkins in the kitchen cupboard.
- Is there a clean cup in the kitchen?
- Yes, there is a clean cup in the kitchen.
- Is the cup red?
- Yes, it is red.

2

Wo ist das Speisezimmer?

Where is the dining room?

A

Vokabeln

1. anschauen - to watch
2. blau - blue
3. braun - brown
4. diese (Fem.) - this (feminine)
5. diese (Pl.) - these (plural)
6. dieser - this (masculine)
7. drei - three
8. Farbe, die - color
9. Fußboden, der; die Etage - floor
10. (her)einkommen - to enter
11. hier - here
12. Kunststoff-, aus Kunststoff - plastic (adj.)

13. leer - empty
14. Messer, das - knife
15. neu - new
16. nicht - not
17. Regal, das - shelf
18. rot - red
19. sechs - six
20. sie (Pl.) - they
21. sitzen - to sit
22. Speisezimmer, das - dining room
23. Spiegel, der - mirror
24. Teppich, der - carpet
25. Vase, die - vase
26. vier - four
27. weiß - white
28. welche(r/s), was für ein(e) - which, what
29. wieviel - how much
30. Zimmer, das - room

B

- Ist das die Küche?
- Ja, das ist die Küche.
- Wo ist das Speisezimmer?
- Das Speisezimmer ist links.
Wir treten in das Speisezimmer ein.
- Was ist das?
- Das ist ein Tisch.
- Ist er aus Kunststoff?
- Nein, er ist hölzern.
- Was gibt es auf dem Tisch?
- Es gibt Teller und Löffel.
- Sind sie sauber?
- Ja, sie sind sauber.
- Was gibt es an dem Tisch?
- Das ist ein Stuhl.
- Ist er neu?

- Is this the kitchen?
- Yes, this is the kitchen.
- Where is the dining room?
- The dining room is to the left.
We enter the dining room.
- What is this?
- This is a table.
- Is it plastic?
- No, it is made of wood.
- What is there on the table?
- These are plates and spoons.
- Are they clean?
- Yes, they are clean.
- What is there at the table?
- This is a chair.
- Is it new?

- Ja, er ist neu und bequem.
- Welche Farbe hat dieser Stuhl?
- Der Stuhl ist braun.
- Wie viele Stühle gibt es in diesem Raum?
- Es gibt vier Stühle in diesem Raum.
- Wo sind die Tassen?
- Die Tassen stehen auf dem Tisch.
- Wo ist der Teekessel?
- Der Teekessel ist auf dem Herd.
- Ist er leer?
- Nein, er ist nicht leer. Die Katze sitzt in dem Teekessel.
- Was hängt auf der Wand?
- Das ist ein Bild.
- Ist das Bild neu oder alt?
- Es ist schön und alt.
- Wo sind die Servietten?
- Die Servietten sind im Schränkchen.
- Wo ist das Schränkchen?
- Es steht in der Nähe des Bildes.
- Welche Farbe hat das Schränkchen?
- Es ist weiß.
- Wie viele Regale gibt es im Schränkchen?
- Das Schränkchen hat drei Regale.
- Wo sind die Gabeln?
- Die Gabeln sind auch im Schränkchen.
- Was ist das?
- Das ist ein Spiegel. Der Hund schaut in den Spiegel.
- Was liegt auf dem Fußboden?

- Yes, it is new and comfortable.
- What color is this chair?
- This chair is brown.
- How many chairs are in this room?
- There are four chairs in this room.
- Where are the cups?
- The cups are on the table.
- Where is the tea kettle?
- The kettle is on the stove.
- Is it empty?
- No, it is not empty. The cat is sitting in the teapot.
- What is hanging on the wall?
- It is a picture.
- Is the picture new or old?
- It is beautiful and old.
- Where are the napkins?
- The napkins are in a cabinet.
- Where is the cabinet?
- It is standing near the picture.
- What color is the cabinet?
- It is white.
- How many shelves are there in the cabinet?
- The cabinet has three shelves.
- Where are the forks?
- The forks are also in the cabinet.
- What is this?
- This is a mirror. The dog is looking in the mirror.
- What's on the floor?

- Das ist ein Teppich.
- Welche Farbe hat der Teppich?
- Der Teppich ist blau.
- Welche Farbe hat die Decke?
- Die Decke ist grau.
- Was hängt unter der Decke?
- Das ist ein Kronleuchter.
- Welche Farbe hat der Kronleuchter?
- Der Kronleuchter ist blau und weiß.
- Wo ist der Kühlschrank?
- Er steht in der Küche.
- Ist der Kühlschrank groß?
- Ja, er ist groß.
- Welche Farbe hat der Kühlschrank?
- Der Kühlschrank ist grau. Die Katze frißt einen Fisch aus dem Kühlschrank.
- Wo ist der Blender?
- Er liegt auf dem Kühlschrank.
- Ist der Blender neu?
- Ja, er ist neu.
- Wo ist die Kaffeemaschine?
- Sie steht neben dem Ausguss.
- Ist die Kaffeemaschine sauber?
- Nein, sie ist schmutzig.
- Wo ist der Toaster?
- Er ist im Küchenregal.
- Was gibt es auf dem Tisch?
- Das ist eine Vase.
- Ist sie gläsern?
- Ja, sie ist gläsern.

- This is a carpet.
- What color is this carpet?
- This carpet is blue.
- What color is the ceiling?
- The ceiling is gray.
- What is hanging on the ceiling?
- This is a chandelier.
- What color is this chandelier?
- This chandelier is blue and white.
- Where is the refrigerator?
- It is located in the kitchen.
- Is the refrigerator big?
- Yes, it's big.
- What color is the refrigerator?
- The refrigerator is gray. The cat is eating fish from the refrigerator.
- Where's the blender?
- It is on the refrigerator.
- Is the blender new?
- Yes, it is new.
- Where is the coffee maker?
- It is near the sink.
- Is the coffee maker clean?
- No, it's dirty.
- Where is the toaster?
- It is in the kitchen cabinet.
- What is there on the table?
- This is a vase.
- Is it glass?
- Yes, it is glass.

- Was steht in der Vase?	- What is standing in the vase?
- Es sind Blumen da.	- These are flowers there.
- Wie viele Blumen gibt es in der Vase?	- How many flowers are there in the vase?
- Es sind sechs Blumen in der Vase.	- There are six flowers in the vase.
- Welche Farbe haben diese Blumen?	- What color are these flowers?
- Sie sind rot.	- They are red.
- Gibt es den Mixer hier?	- Is there the mixer here?
- Nein, der Mixer ist in der Küche.	- No, the mixer is in the kitchen.
- Gibt es Messer im Schränkchen?	- Are there knives in the cabinet?
- Ja, es sind Messer im Schränkchen.	- Yes, there are knives in the cabinet.
- Welche Farbe hat dieser Teller?	- What color is this dish?
- Er ist blau.	- It is blue.
- Welche Farbe hat diese Wand?	- What color is this wall?
- Sie ist grün.	- It is green.

3

Der Saal

The hall

 **A**

Vokabeln

1. arbeiten, funktionieren - to work, function
2. auch - also
3. bei, an - at, near
4. beigefarben, beige (unflektiert), sandfarbig - beige
5. Buch, das - book
6. Fernseher, der - tv-set
7. Foto, das - photograph
8. geradeaus - straight
9. interessant - interesting
10. Kamin, der - fireplace
11. Kissen, das - pillow
12. Lampe, die - lamp
13. liegen - to lie
14. mehr, noch - more, still
15. nah - near

16. ob - whether, if
17. purpurrot - purple
18. Rose, die - rose
19. Rundfunk, der; das Radio - radio
20. Saal, der; die Halle - hall, auditorium
21. Schalter, der - switch
22. schwarz - black
23. Sessel, der - armchair
24. Shakespeare - Shakespeare
25. Sofa, das - sofa, couch
26. Tischlein, das - caffee table, little table
27. Tulpe, die - tulip
28. unter - under
29. vergehen - to pass
30. viele - many, a lot
31. weich - soft

B

- Wo ist der Saal?

- Der Saal ist geradeaus.

Wir treten in den Saal ein. Der Raum ist groß und gemütlich. Die Decke ist grau. Die Wände sind grün.

- Was gibt es auf dem Fußboden?

- Ein Teppich liegt auf dem Fußboden. Er ist weich. Der Teppich ist purpurrot.

- Was steht auf dem Teppich?

- Es gibt ein Tischlein auf dem Teppich. Es ist aus Glas. Ein interessantes Buch liegt auf dem Tischlein. Es ist grau.

- Wo ist der Sessel?

- Der Sessel steht hinter dem Tischlein. Er ist groß und bequem.

- Gibt es ein Sofa in diesem Raum?

- Ja, ein Sofa steht in der Nähe des Fensters. Eine Katze sitzt auf dem Sofa mit dem Fisch. Kissen liegen auch auf dem Sofa. Sie sind purpurrot. Die Kissen sind weich und

- Where is the hall?

- The hall is straight ahead.

We pass into the hall. The room is large and cozy. The ceiling is gray. The walls are green.

- What is there on the floor?

- On the floor there is a carpet. It is soft. The carpet is purple.

- What is standing on the carpet?

- There is a small table on the carpet. It is glass. On the table there is an interesting book. It is gray.

- Where is the armchair?

- The armchair is behind the small table. It is large and comfortable.

- Is there a sofa in this room?

- Yes, the sofa stands near a window. A cat is sitting on the couch with fish. There are couch cushions lying on the couch as well. They are purple. The pillows are soft

bequem.

- Was hängt an der Wand?

- Ein Bild hängt an der Wand.

- Wo ist der Kamin in diesem Raum?

- Der Kamin ist unter dem Bild. Er ist groß und schön.

- Was gibt es auf dem Sims?

- Es gibt ein Foto und eine Vase auf dem Sims.

- Was gibt es in der Vase?

- Es gibt schöne gelbe Rosen in der Vase.

- Wie viele Rosen gibt es in der Vase?

- Es gibt sechs Rosen in der Vase.

- Gibt es mehr Blumen in diesem Raum?

- Ja, es gibt Tulpen auf der Fensterbank.

- Gibt es Bücher in diesem Raum?

- Ja, es gibt viele Bücher im Bücherschrank.

- Wo ist das Bücherschrank?

- Es steht in der Nähe der Tür.

- Was gibt es in dem Bücherschrank?

- Es gibt Bücher und Fotos im Bücherschrank.

- Gibt es Bücher von Shakespeare im Schrank?

- Ja, sie sind rot.

- Wie viele Regale gibt es im Bücherschrank?

- Es gibt vier Regale im Bücherschrank.

- Was gibt es auf der Decke?

- Ein neuer Kronleuchter hängt von der Decke.

- Wo ist der Schalter?

and comfortable.

- What is hanging on the wall?

- A picture is hanging on the wall.

- Where is the fireplace in this room?

- The fireplace is located under the picture. It is big and beautiful.

- What is there on the mantelpiece?

- There is a photo and a vase on the mantelpiece.

- What is in the vase?

- There are beautiful yellow roses in the vase.

- How many roses are there in the vase?

- There are six roses in the vase.

- Are there more flowers in this room?

- Yes, there are tulips on the windowsill.

- Are there books in this room?

- Yes, there are a lot of books in the bookcase.

- Where is the bookcase?

- It is located near the door.

- What is there in the bookcase?

- There are books and photographs in the bookcase.

- Are there books by Shakepseare in the bookcase?

- Yes, they are red.

- How many shelves are there in the bookcase?

- In the bookcase there are four shelves.

- What is there on the ceiling?

- There is a new chandelier on the ceiling.

- Der Schalter ist auf der Wand auf der rechten Seite.
- Gibt es mehr Lampen in diesem Raum?
- Es gibt noch eine Lampe neben dem Sofa.
- Welche Farbe hat diese Lampe?
- Sie ist beige.
- Hast du einen Fernseher?
- Ja, er ist in der Ecke.
- Ist der Fernseher groß oder klein?
- Er ist groß und schwarz.
- Funktioniert dieses Radio?
- Ja, es funktioniert.

- Where's the switch?
- The switch is on the wall on the right.
- Are there more lamps in the room?
- There is another lamp near the sofa.
- What color is this lamp?
- It is beige.
- Do you have a TV?
- Yes, it is in the corner.
- Is the TV big or small?
- It's big and black.
- Does this radio work?
- Yes, it works.

4

Das Badezimmer

The bathroom

 A

Vokabeln

1. Badewanne, die - bathtub
2. Badezimmer, das; das Bad - bathroom
3. Bürste, die - brush
4. Dusche, die - shower
5. essen - to eat
6. Essen, das - food
7. Hand, die - hand
8. Handtuch, das - towel
9. heiß - hot
10. hören - to listen to
11. Korb, der - basket

12. kühl - cold
13. Läufer, der; der Bettvorleger - little rug, mat
14. lesen - to read
15. machen - to make
16. Maschine, die - machine
17. mit - with
18. möglich - possible
19. Müll, der; der Abfall - trash, garbage
20. neben - next to, near
21. nehmen - to take (a shower, medicine etc.)
22. Papier, das - paper
23. reinigen, sauber machen - to clean
24. Seife, die - soap
25. sich ausruhen, sich erholen - to rest, to relax
26. sich waschen - to wash oneself
27. sprechen, plaudern - to talk, to chat
28. Toilette, die - toilet (bowl)
29. Toiletten- - toilet, bathroom (adj.)
30. Wasch- (z.B. Waschpulver) - laundry, washing (adj.)
31. Waschbecken, das - washbasin
32. Wäsche, die; die Unterwäsche - laundry, underwear, linen
33. waschen - to wash, to clean
34. Wasserhahn, der - faucet, tap
35. Zahn- - tooth (adj.)
36. Zähne, die (Pl.) - teeth
37. zubereiten - to prepare, to cook

B

Wir gehen weiter ins Badezimmer. Das Bad ist klein und hell. Die Wände im Badezimmer sind blau. Die Decke ist weiß.

- Was ist das?

- Das ist die Badewanne.

- Ist sie aus Kunststoff oder aus Metall?

- Die Badewanne ist aus Kunststoff.

- Was gibt es über der Badewanne?

- Das ist der Wasserhahn und die Dusche. Es gibt einen Hahn mit warmem und mit kaltem Wasser.

- Was hängt an der Wand?

- Das ist ein sauberes Handtuch. Es ist blau.

- Was liegt neben der Badewanne auf dem

We proceed to the bathroom. The bathroom is small and bright. The walls in the bathroom are blue. The ceiling is white.

- What is this?

- This is the bathtub.

- Is it plastic or metal?

- The tub is plastic.

- What is there above the bathtub?

- This is a faucet and shower. There is a tap with hot and with cold water.

- What is hanging on the wall?

- This is a clean towel. It is blue.

- What is lying near the bathtub on the

Fußboden?	floor?
- Ein Läufer liegt neben der Badewanne.	- A mat is lying near the bathtub.
- Was gibt es rechts?	- What is there on the right?
- Das ist ein Waschbecken. Über dem Waschbecken hängt ein Spiegel. Es gibt auch einen Hahn mit warmem und kaltem Wasser.	- This is a washbasin. There is a mirror hanging over the washbasin. There is also a tap with hot and cold water.
- Was gibt es auf dem Waschbecken?	- What is there on the sink?
- Auf dem Waschbecken gibt es Seife und Zahnbürsten.	- On the sink, there are soap and toothbrushes.
- Was gibt es neben dem Waschbecken?	- What is near the sink?
- Das ist eine Waschmaschine. Sie ist weiß. Die Waschmaschine ist neu.	- It is a washing machine. It is white. The washing machine is new.
- Was gibt es neben der Waschmaschine?	- What is there near the washing machine?
- Neben der Waschmaschine steht ein Korb mit schmutziger Wäsche.	- There is a basket for dirty laundry near the washing machine.
- Was gibt es in der Ecke?	- What is there in the corner?
- In der Ecke steht ein Mülleimer.	- There is a trash can in the corner.
- Was gibt es hinter dem Waschbecken?	- What is behind the wash basin?
- Hinter dem Waschbecken gibt es eine Toilette.	- There is a toilet behind the washbasin.
- Was gibt es neben der Toilette?	- What is near the toilet bowl?
- Das ist Toilettenpapier und eine Toilettenbürste.	- This is toilet paper and a toilet brush.
- Was kann man im Badezimmer machen?	- What can you do in the bathroom?
- Im Badezimmer kann man die Hände waschen, sich waschen, ein Bad nehmen oder die Zähne putzen.	- In the bathroom you can wash your hands, wash, bath, and brush your teeth.
- Was kann man in der Küche machen?	- What can you do in the kitchen?
- In der Küche kann man Essen zubereiten und das Geschirr waschen.	- In the kitchen you can cook food and wash dishes.
- Was kann man im Speisezimmer machen?	- What can you do in the dining room?
- Im Speisezimmer kann man essen und sprechen.	- In the dining room, you can eat and talk.

- Was kann man im Wohnzimmer machen?

- Im Wohnzimmer kann man sich erholen, fernsehen, Rundfunk hören, lesen oder sprechen.

- What can you do in the living room?

- In the living room, you can relax, watch TV, listen to the radio, talk, read.

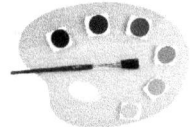

5

Kannst du Deutsch oder Spanisch sprechen?

Can you speak German or Spanish?

A

Vokabeln

1. abends, am Abend - in the evening
2. aber - but
3. andere(r/s) - other
4. anrufen - to call (by phone)
5. Arbeit, die - work
6. auf Deutsch - in German
7. auf Englisch - in English
8. auf Französisch - in French
9. auf Spanisch - in Spanish
10. aufräumen - to clean, to tidy up
11. Basketball, der - basketball
12. Baum, der - tree
13. brauchen - to be necessary, to need to
14. Bruder, der - brother
15. Café, das - cafe

16. Computer, der - computer
17. dein - your(s)
18. du, Sie - you
19. ein bisschen - a bit, a little
20. Englisch - English
21. Französisch - French (adj.)
22. Freund, der - friend
23. gehen - to go, to walk
24. Geschäft, das; der Laden - store, shop
25. gut - well
26. Heft, das - notebook, copybook
27. helfen - to help
28. heute - today
29. ich - I
30. ihn, sein - him, his
31. jetzt - now
32. Kino, das - cinema, movie theater
33. können - to be able to, can
34. krank werden, erkranken - to get sick
35. legen - to put (down)
36. lehren, beibringen - to teach
37. mein - my
38. mein, dein etc. (eigen) - someone's (own)
39. morgen - tomorrow
40. nach - after
41. nach Hause - homeward
42. nehmen - to take
43. rufen, nennen - to call, to name
44. schreiben - to write
45. sein - to be
46. sich bemühen - to work hard
47. sollen - to have to, to be obliged
48. spielen - to play
49. Sprache, die; die Zunge - language, tongue
50. sprechen - to speak
51. Telefon, das - phone
52. unser - our(s)
53. vielleicht - maybe
54. wahrscheinlich - probably
55. warten - to wait
56. warum - why

 B

1

- Kannst du Englisch oder Französisch lesen?
- Ich kann beide auf Englisch und auf Französisch lesen und schreiben.
- Kannst du diese Sprachen sprechen?
- Ich spreche ein bisschen Englisch. Ich kann

1

- Can you read in English or in French?
- I can read and write in English and in French.
- Can you speak these languages?
- I can speak a little English. I do not

Französisch nicht sprechen.

- Kannst du Deutsch oder Spanisch sprechen?
- Ja, ich spreche Deutsch und Spanisch gut.
- Kannst du mich Spanisch lehren?
- Ja, ich kann. Aber du musst dich bemühen.

2

- Kannst du Basketball spielen?
- Nein, aber ich kann es lernen.
- Vielleicht spielen wir morgen?
- Morgen kann ich nicht, aber ich kann heute spielen.
- Vielleicht heute Abend?
- Ja, ich kann am Abend spielen. Kannst du deine Freunde anrufen?
- Ja, ich kann.

3

- Wo ist dein Bruder?
- Wir müssen auf ihn warten.
- Wahrscheinlich wird er nicht kommen. Kann ich nach Hause gehen?
- Ja, du kannst.

4

- Kann ich dieses Buch nehmen?
- Nein, du kannst dieses Buch nicht nehmen.
- Kann ich diese Tasse nehmen?
- Nein, du kannst diese Tasse nicht nehmen. Du kannst eine andere Tasse aus der Küche nehmen.
- Wo ist dein Freund?
- Er ist wahrscheinlich draußen.

speak French.

- Can you speak German or Spanish?
- Yes, I speak German and Spanish well.
- Can you teach me how to speak Spanish?
- Yes, I can. But you have to work.

2

- Can you play basketball?
- No, but I can learn.
- Maybe we'll play tomorrow?
- I can't tomorrow, but today I can.
- Maybe tonight?
- Yes, I can play in the evening. Can you call your friends?
- Yes, I can.

3

- Where is your brother?
- We have to wait for him.
- He probably will not come. Can I go home?
- Yes, you can.

4

- Can I take this book?
- No, you may not take this book.
- Can I take this cup?
- No, you may not take this cup. You can take another cup from the kitchen.
- Where is your friend?
- He's probably outside.

5

Ich werde wahrscheinlich ins Kino gehen. Kannst du mitkommen?

- Nein, ich kann nicht. Ich muss arbeiten.

- Vielleicht kannst du nach der Arbeit gehen?

- Ja, ich kann nach der Arbeit gehen.

- Wo ist mein Buch?

- Es ist wahrscheinlich in dem Bücherschrank.

- Kann ich deinen Kugelschreiber nehmen?

- Ja, du kannst einen Kugelschreiber aus dem Bücherschrank nehmen.

6

- Kann ich dieses Heft nehmen?

- Nein, du kannst dieses Heft nicht nehmen.

- Kann ich mich am Tisch setzen?

- Ja, du kannst.

- Kann ich meinen Heft hier legen?

- Ja, du kannst.

- Kann ich jetzt Computerspiele spielen?

- Ja, du kannst jetzt spielen.

- Ich muss jetzt telefonieren. Kann ich dieses Telefon nehmen?

- Ja, du kannst es nehmen.

- Können wir zum Café gehen?

- Nein, ich muss arbeiten gehen.

7

- Wo ist unsere Katze?

- Sie ist wahrscheinlich auf dem Baum.

- Vielleicht ist sie zu Hause?

- Nein, sie ist nicht zu Hause.

5

- I'll probably go to the movies. Can you come with me?

- No, I can't. I have to do work.

- Maybe you go after work?

- Yes, I can go after work.

- Where is my book?

- It's probably in the bookcase.

- Can I take your pen?

- Yes, you can take a pen from the bookcase.

6

- Can I take this notebook?

- No, you may not take this notebook.

- Can I sit down at the table?

- Yes, you can.

- Can I put my notebook here?

- Yes, you can.

- Can I play computer games now?

- Yes, you can play now.

- I need to phone now. Can I take this phone?

- Yes, you can take it.

- Can we go to the cafe?

- No, I have to go to work.

7

- Where is our cat?

- He's probably in the tree.

- Maybe he's in the house?

- No, he is not in the house.

8

- Warum ist dein Freund nicht gekommen?
- Er ist wahrscheinlich krank.
- Du musst jetzt das Wohnzimmer aufräumen.
- Vielleicht kannst du mir helfen?
- Nein, ich muss das Geschirr waschen.

9

- Wo sind die Zahnbürsten?
- Vielleicht liegen sie auf der Waschmaschine.
- Wo ist mein rotes Heft?
- Es ist wahrscheinlich auf dem Sofa.
- Vielleicht kannst du mit mir zum Geschäft gehen?
- Ja, ich kann mitgehen.

8

- Why did your friend not come?
- He's probably sick.
- You have to clean the living room now.
- Maybe you will help me?
- No, I have to wash the dishes.

9

- Where are the toothbrushes?
- Maybe they are on the washing machine.
- Where is my red notebook?
- It's probably on the couch.
- Maybe you'll come with me to the store?
- Yes, I can go.

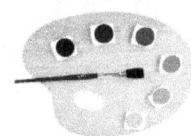

6

Kannst du mir helfen?

Can you help me?

A

Vokabeln

1. Abenteuer, das - adventure
2. aber, doch, und - but, while, and
3. alles - all
4. aufschreiben - to write (down)
5. Brille, die - glasses
6. damals, dann - then
7. Detektiv, der - detective
8. diese (Sing.) - that (feminine)
9. dort - there (place)
10. einschalten - to turn on
11. fahren - to ride
12. finden - to find
13. Frau, die - woman
14. frei - free

15. fünf - five
16. Fußball- - soccer (adj.)
17. Garage, die - garage
18. gefallen - to like, to appeal
19. gehen - to walk, to go
20. haben - to have, to own
21. ihr - your(s) (plural)
22. Italiener, der - Italian (person)
23. Jahr, das - year
24. Katze, die - cat
25. Kleidung, die - clothing, robe
26. leben - to live
27. Licht, das - light
28. Liebe, die - love
29. lieben - to love
30. Mann, der - man
31. mein - my (mine)
32. Milch, das - milk
33. Motorrad, das - motorcycle, motorbike
34. Mutter, die Mama - Mom
35. Nachbar, der - neighbor
36. natürlich - of course
37. nicht neu - not new
38. Nummer, die - number
39. Papa, der - Dad
40. Polizei, die - police
41. Sammlung, die - collection
42. Schwester, die - sister
43. sehen - to see
44. sie (Sing.) - her
45. sie, ihr (Pl.) - them, their(s)
46. Spanier, der - Spaniard
47. Tee, der - tea
48. Telefon- - telephone (adj.)
49. Tourist, der - tourist
50. trinken - to drink
51. über - about, over, along
52. wegfahren - to go/ride away
53. wenig - little, few
54. wer - who
55. wessen - whose
56. wie viele Jahre - how many years
57. Zeit, die - time

B

1

- Kann ich dein Heft nehmen?

- Ja, du kannst. Es ist auf dem Tisch. Mein Heft ist blau.

- Ich kann es nicht finden.

- Vielleicht ist mein Heft auf dem Sofa.

1

- Can I take your notebook?

- Yes, you can. It is on the table. My notebook is blue.

- I cannot find it.

- Maybe my notebook is on the couch.

- Ja, es ist auf dem Sofa.

- Hast du noch einen Kugelschreiber? Ich muss eine Telefonnummer aufschreiben.

- Mein Kugelschreiber liegt auf dem Tisch. Er ist aus Metall.

2

- Wie alt ist eure Katze?

- Unsere Katze ist fünf Jahre alt.

- Was frißt eure Katze am liebsten?

- Unsere Katze mag Milch trinken.

- Wie alt ist ihre Katze?

- Ihre Katze ist drei Jahre alt.

3

- Hast du viele Freunde?

- Ja, ich habe viele Freunde.

- Ich habe keine Freunde in dieser Stadt.

- Vielleicht werde ich am Abend mit meinen Freunden ins Kino gehen. Kannst du mitkommen?

- Ja, ich kann.

- Kann deine Schwester auch mitkommen?

- Ich kann sie anrufen.

- Ich werde dich am Abend anrufen.

- Wohnen deine Freunde in dieser Stadt?

- Ja, alle meine Freunde wohnen in dieser Stadt.

4

- Ich muss das Zimmer aufräumen. Kannst du mir helfen?

- Nein, ich muss mein Telefon finden.

- Vielleicht ist dein Telefon in der Küche.

- Hilf mir, mein Telefon zu finden und ich

- Yes, it's on the couch.

- Do you have another pen? I need to write down a phone number.

- My pen is on the table. It's metal.

2

- How old is your cat?

- Our cat is five years old.

- What does your cat like to eat?

- Our cat likes to drink milk.

- How old is her cat?

- Her cat is three years old.

3

- Do you have many friends?

- Yes, I have many friends.

- I have no friends in this town.

- Maybe in the evening we will go to the movies with my friends. Can you come with us?

- Yes, I can.

- Will your sister go with us?

- I can call her.

- I'll call you in the evening.

- Do your friends live in this city?

- Yes, all of my friends live in this city.

4

- I have to clean the room. Can you help me?

- No, I need to find my phone.

- Perhaps your phone is in the kitchen.

- Help me find my phone, and I'll help you

werde dir mit dem Saubermachen helfen.

5
- Hast du irgendwelche interessanten Bücher?
- Ich habe eine große Buchsammlung. Viele meiner Bücher sind über Abenteuer. Ich habe auch Bücher über Liebe.
- Hast du Detektivromane?
- Ja, einige.
- Kann ich sie sehen?
- Ja, du kannst. Sie sind im Regal. In dem Regal rechts.
- Meine Mutter hat auch eine Büchersammlung.

6
- Ich muss Papas Brille finden. Wo ist sie?
- Vielleicht ist seine Brille im Regal.
- Nein, seine Brille ist nicht dort.
- Dann ist sie im Zimmer auf dem Tisch.
- Ich habe die Brille gefunden.

7
- Ich muss unsere Tassen waschen.
- Musst du die Tassen jetzt waschen?
- Ja, ich muss sie jetzt waschen.
- Gibt es saubere Tassen in diesem Zimmer?
- Ja, es gibt mehrere saubere Tassen in diesem Regal.
- Welche Tasse ist für mich?
- Deine Tasse ist gelb, aber meine ist blau.

8
- Dieser Mann ist mein Papa. Das ist Papas Haus.

clean the room.

5
- Do you have any interesting books?
- I have a large collection of books. Many of my books are about adventures. I have also books about love.
- Do you have detective books?
- Yes, a few.
- Can I see them?
- Yes, you can. They are on the shelf. On the shelf on the right.
- My mother also has a collection of books.

6
- I need to find Dad's glasses. Where are they?
- Maybe his glasses are on the shelf.
- No, his glasses are not there.
- Then they are in the room on the table.
- I found his glasses.

7
- I have to wash our cups.
- You have to wash the cups now?
- Yes, I have to wash them now.
- Are there clean cups in this room?
- Yes, there are many clean cups on that shelf.
- Which cup is mine?
- Your cup is yellow, but mine is blue.

8
- This man is my dad. This is Dad's home.

- Ist sein Haus neu?

- Nein, es ist nicht neu.

- Ist das dein Auto?

- Nein, dass ist ein blaues Auto, und unser Auto ist rot.

9

- Das ist meine Mutter.

- Geht sie weg?

- Ja, sie geht arbeiten.

- Ist das ihr Auto?

- Ja, das ist das Auto meiner Mutter. Ihr Auto ist neu.

- Hat dein Papa auch ein Auto?

- Ja, sein Auto steht in der Garage.

10

- Magst du Hunde?

- Nein, aber meine Mutter hat einen Hund.

- Gehört dieser Hund deiner Mutti?

- Ja, das ist ihr Hund.

11

- Wo ist dein Zimmer?

- Mein Zimmer ist rechts. Es ist sauber und hell.

- Wessen Zimmer ist links?

- Das ist das Zimmer meiner Mutter. Ihr Zimmer ist groß und schön.

12

- Gibt es Wasser im Teekessel?

- Ja, es gibt ein wenig Wasser im Teekessel.

- Kann ich mir Tee machen?

- Ja, natürlich.

- Is his house new?

- No, it is not new.

- Is this your car?

- No, this is a blue car, and our car is red.

9

- This is my mom.

- Is she leaving?

- Yes, she is going to work.

- Is this her car?

- Yes, this is my mother's car. Her car is new.

- Does your dad also have a car?

- Yes, his car is in the garage.

10

- Do you like dogs?

- No, but my mom has a dog.

- This dog is your mother's?

- Yes, it is her dog.

11

- Where is your room?

- My room on the right. It is clean and bright.

- Whose room is on the left?

- This is my mother's room. Her room is big and beautiful.

12

- Is there water in the kettle?

- Yes, there is a little water in the kettle.

- Can I make some tea?

- Yes, of course.

13

- Unsere Katze hat nur ein wenig Milch getrunken.
- Ich denke dass sie krank war.

14

- Gibt es viele Italiener und Spanier in dieser Stadt?
- Ja, es gibt viele Touristen hier.
- Unsere Stadt ist schön.
- Ich mag es, hier zu leben.

15

- Wer ist das?
- Das ist mein Freund, Robert.
- Er hat alte Kleidung.
- Er mag das Einkaufen nicht.

16

- Wohnt diese Frau in dem Haus gegenüber?
- Ja, sie ist unsere Nachbarin.
- Ist das ihr Motorrad?
- Ja, das ist ihr Motorrad.

17

- Es gibt wenig Licht in diesem Zimmer. Kannst du das Licht einschalten?
- Ja, ich kann.

18

- Gibt es heute viele Polizisten in der Stadt?
- Ja, heute gibt es ein Fußballspiel.
- Vielleicht können wir zum Fußballspiel gehen?
- Ja, ich habe viel Freizeit.

13

- Our cat drank just a little milk.
- I think she was ill.

14

- Are there many Italians and Spaniards in this city?
- Yes, there are a lot of tourists.
- Our city is beautiful.
- I like living here.

15

- Who's that?
- This is my friend Robert.
- His clothes are old.
- He does not like to shop.

16

- This woman lives in a house across the street?
- Yes, she is our neighbor.
- Is that her motorcycle there?
- Yes, it's her motorcycle.

17

- In this room, there is little light. Can you turn on the light?
- Yes, I can.

18

- Are there many policemen in the city today?
- Yes, today is the football game.
- Maybe we'll go to a football match?
- Yes, I have a lot of free time.

7

Wie heißt du?

What's your name?

A

Vokabeln

1. acht - eight
2. achtzehn - eighteen
3. Agentur, die; das Büro - agency
4. älter - older
5. Arzt, der - doctor, physician
6. Auto, das; der Wagen - automobile, car
7. Autoservice, der - car service
8. Beruf, der; das Fach - profession
9. bis - until, to
10. Briefmarke, die - stamp

11. Deutsch - German
12. dreißig - thirty
13. du, Sie - you
14. ein - one
15. Eltern, die - parents
16. England - England
17. Engländerin, die - Englishwoman
18. fahren - to ride, to go
19. Familie, die - family
20. Frank - Frank
21. Fußball, der - soccer
22. Fußballspieler, der - soccer player
23. ganze - whole
24. Gast, der - guest
25. geboren sein - to be born
26. Großbritannien - Great Britain
27. Hallo - hi, hello
28. Haus-, häuslich - house/home (adj.)
29. herrlich - excellent
30. immer - always
31. Immobilie, die; das Grundbesitz - real estate
32. irgendwelcher - any, some
33. Italien - Italy
34. Jahre - years
35. kalt, kühl - cold
36. Keks, der; das Törtchen - cookie
37. kennen - to know
38. kennenlernen - to get acquainted, to learn
39. Kinder- - children's (adj.), child (adj.)
40. Kinderkrippe - nursery
41. Klub, der - club
42. Lachs, der - salmon
43. Land, das - country
44. Leben, das - life
45. lernen - to study, to learn
46. letztens, kürzlich - not long ago, recently
47. Londoner - London (adj.)
48. Mechaniker, der - mechanic
49. national - national
50. Nationalität, die - nationality
51. Neapel - Naples
52. oft - often
53. Philip - Philip
54. Pizza, die - pizza
55. Postamt, das - post office
56. professionell - professional
57. reisen - to travel
58. Renovierung, die - renovation, repairs
59. Schriftstellerin, die - writer (fem.)
60. Schule, die - school
61. sehr - very
62. Speise, die; das Gericht - dish
63. Tier, das - animal
64. Universität, die - university
65. uns - us
66. Urlaub, der; die Ferien - vacation
67. Vater, der - father
68. verkaufen - to sell

69. vierzig - forty
70. wann, als - when
71. wie - how
72. woher - from where

73. zu, nach - to
74. zwanzig - twenty
75. zwei - two
76. zwölf - twelve

B

1

- Hallo.
- Hallo. Wie heißt du?
- Ich heiße Frank. Und du?
- Ich heiße Mario.
- Wie alt bist du?
- Ich bin achtzehn Jahre alt.
- Welcher Nationalität bist du?
- Ich bin in Großbritannien geboren und ich lebe dort. Mein Vater ist Spanier und meine Mutter Engländerin. Und woher bist du?
- Ich bin Italiener. Ich wohne in Neapel. Arbeitest du oder studierst?
- Ich studiere an der Nationalen Universität. Und was bist du von Beruf?
- Ich bin Mechaniker. Ich habe einen eigenen Autoservice in Italien.
- Magst du England?
- Ich mag dieses Land, aber es ist kalt hier. Ich reise jetzt viel. Magst du reisen?
- Ich reise gern, aber jetzt habe ich sehr wenig Zeit.
- Könntest du mich mit deiner Familie besuchen?
- Ich kann nicht. Jetzt muss ich viel lernen.

1

- Hi.
- Hi. What's your name?
- My name is Frank. And what's your name?
- My name is Mario.
- How old are you?
- I'm eighteen years old.
- What is your nationality?
- I was born and live in Great Britain. My dad is a Spaniard. My mother is an Englishwoman. And where are you from?
- I'm Italian by nationality. I live in Naples. Do you work or study?
- I am a student at the National University. And what is your profession?
- I am a mechanic. I have my own car service in Italy.
- Do you like England?
- I like this country, but it's cold here. I now travel a lot. Do you like to travel?
- I like to travel, but now I have very little time.
- Could you come visit me with your family?
- I cannot. Now I have to study a lot.

2

- Hast du immer in diesem Haus gewohnt?
- Ja, ich habe mein ganzes Leben lang hier gewohnt.
- Du hast ein schönes Haus!
- Ja, wir hatten kürzlich eine Renovierung.
- Du hast viele schönen Blumen im Garten.
- Ja, meine Mutter mag Blumen.

3

- Vielleicht trinken wir Tee?
- Ja, lass uns in die Küche gehen.
- Hast du schwarzen Tee?
- Ja, wir haben schwarzen und grünen Tee.
- Welches Essen magst du am besten?
- Ich mag es, wenn meine Mutter Speisen mit Lachs zubereitet. Sie macht auch gute Kekse.
- Ich esse Pizza wirklich gern.
- Kannst du Pizza machen?
- Ja, ich kann. Ich mag kochen.

4

- Hast du Haustiere?
- Ja, ich habe einen Hund. Er heißt Johnny.
- Wie alt ist er?
- Er ist sechs Jahre alt.
- Ich habe auch einen Hund in Italien.

5

- Kannst du gut Deutsch sprechen?
- Ja, ich habe es mit meinem Vater gelernt. Spricht jeder Deutsch in deiner Familie?
- Ja, wir sprechen alle Deutsch.

2

- Have you always lived in this house?
- Yes, I've lived here all my life.
- You have a beautiful home!
- Yes, we recently made repairs.
- You have a lot of beautiful flowers in the garden.
- Yes, my mom likes flowers.

3

- Maybe we can drink tea?
- Yes, let's go to the kitchen.
- Do you have black tea?
- Yes, we have black and green tea.
- What food do you like?
- I like it when my mom prepares dishes with salmon. She also makes good cookies.
- And I really like pizza.
- Can you cook pizza?
- Yes, I can. I like cooking.

4

- Do you have any pets?
- Yes, I have a dog. His name is Johnny.
- How old is he?
- He's six years old.
- I also have a dog in Italy.

5

- Can you speak German well?
- Yes, I have learned it with my father. Does everyone speak German in your family?
- Yes, we all speak German.

- Kennst du auch eine andere Sprache?

- Ich kann ein bisschen Französisch sprechen.

6

- Gehört das Buch auf dem Tisch dir?

- Ja, das ist mein Buch. Das sind Detektiverzählungen von Agatha Christie. Magst du diese Autorin?

- Ja. Sie schreibt tolle Detektivromane.

- Liest du gerne?

- Ja. Ich lese sehr viel.

7

- Hast du eine große Familie?

- Ja, ich habe eine große Familie. Ich habe einen Vater, eine Mutter, zwei Brüder und eine kleine Schwester.

- Wie alt ist deine Schwester?

- Sie ist ein Jahr alt.

- Wie heißt sie?

- Sie heißt Joe. Sie kann noch nicht laufen.

- Wo ist deine Schwester jetzt?

- Sie ist in der Kinderkrippe.

- Was ist dein Vater von Beruf?

- Er ist Arzt von Beruf. Aber jetzt arbeitet er nicht.

- Warum?

- Er macht jetzt Urlaub.

- Wo arbeitet deine Mutter?

- Sie arbeitet in einem Immobilienbüro. Sie verkauft Häuser.

- Wie lang arbeitet sie dort?

- Sie arbeitet dort seit acht Jahren.

- Do you know another language?

- I speak a little French.

6

- Is this book on the table yours?

- Yes, this book is mine. These are detective stories by Agatha Christie. Do you like this author?

- Yes. She writes excellent detective stories.

- Do you like to read?

- Yes. I read a lot.

7

- Do you have a big family?

- Yes, I have a big family. I have a father, mother, two brothers and a little sister.

- How old is your sister?

- She is one year old.

- What's her name?

- Her name is Joe. She still does not know how to walk.

- Where is your sister now?

- She's at the nursery.

- What is your father's profession?

- He is a doctor by profession. But now he is not working.

- Why?

- He's on vacation.

- Where does your mom work?

- She works in a real estate agency. She sells houses.

- How long has she been working there?

- She has been working there for eight

- Wo arbeitete sie früher?
- Sie arbeitete in einem Postamt.
- Ist sie jetzt im Büro?
- Nein, sie ist im Geschäft.
- Wie alt sind deine Eltern?
- Meine Mutter ist achtunddreißig Jahre alt. Mein Vater ist einundvierzig.
- Sind es deine Brüder in diesem Bild?
- Ja.
- Wie heißen sie?
- Das ist Philip. Er ist zwölf Jahre alt.
- Lernt er in der Schule?
- Ja, er besucht die Schule.
- Hat er gute Noten?
- Ja, er hat gute Noten.
- Und wer ist das?
- Das ist mein älterer Bruder John.
- Wie alt ist er?
- Er ist einundzwanzig Jahre alt.
- Arbeitet er?
- Ja, er ist ein professioneller Fußballspieler.
- Ich mag Fußball. In welchem Klub spielt er?
- Er spielt im Londoner Klub.
- Kann ich ihn kennenlernen?
- Ja, natürlich.

8

- Hast du ein Auto?
- Ja, wir haben ein neues Auto.
- Was für ein Auto habt ihr?

- Where did she work before?
- She worked at the post office.
- Is she at work now?
- No, she's at the store.
- How old are your parents?
- My mom is thirty-eight years old. My dad is forty-one years old.
- Are these your brothers in the photo?
- Yes.
- What are their names?
- This is Philip. He is twelve years old.
- Is he learning?
- Yes, he goes to school.
- Does he get good notes?
- Yes, he gets good notes.
- And who is this?
- This is my older brother John.
- How old is he?
- He is twenty-one years old.
- Is he working?
- Yes, he is a professional soccer player.
- I like soccer. Which club does he play in?
- He plays in the London club.
- Can I meet him?
- Yes, of course.

8

- Do you have a car?
- Yes, we have a new car.
- What car do you have?

- Wir haben eine BMW.

- Fährt ihr oft Auto?

- Ja, meine Mutter fährt oft mit dem Auto zur Arbeit.

- We have a BMW.

- Do you drive it often?

- Yes, my mother often drives it to work.

8

Der Weg zur Universität
The way to university

 A

Vokabeln

1. abschneiden - to cut off
2. alles - everything
3. Apfel, der - apple
4. aufstehen - to get up
5. belegte Brot, das; die Schnitte - sandwich
6. bezahlen - to pay
7. Brot, das - bread
8. Brücke, die - bridge
9. Cerealien, die - flakes, cereal
10. dann - afterwards, then
11. dort(hin) - there (direction)
12. ein Stückchen - a little piece
13. (ein)giessen - to pour in
14. einige - a few, some
15. erreichen - to arrive, get to
16. Euro, der - Euro

17. Fahrt, die - passage; fare
18. frühstücken, Frühstück essen - to have breakfast
19. gießen - to pour (something fluid)
20. gut - good
21. Haltestelle, die - stop
22. (hin)ausgehen - to go out, get out
23. (hin)zufügen - to add
24. Honig, der - honey
25. in der Mitte - in the middle
26. jeder - every
27. Kaffee, der - coffee
28. Käse, der - cheese
29. Kino, das - cinema, movie theater
30. kosten - to cost
31. legen - to put
32. Leute, die - people
33. machen, schaffen - to do (finish)
34. manchmal - sometimes
35. Minibus, der - minibus
36. Minute, die - minute
37. Morgen, der - morning
38. Museum, das - museum
39. neun - nine
40. nicht weit - not far
41. normalerweise - normally, usually
42. nötig - necessary
43. Oberleitungsbus, der; der Obus - trolleybus
44. öffnen, aufmachen - to open
45. ohne - without
46. Ort, der; der Platz - place
47. Park, der - park
48. (Platz) nehmen - to occupy
49. sammeln - to collect, to gather
50. schneiden - to cut
51. schon - already
52. schütten - to pour (something loose)
53. See, der - lake
54. sich setzen - to sit down
55. sich versammeln - to gather together
56. sieben - seven
57. so dass - in order to, so that
58. stehen - to stand
59. stellen, legen - to put (vertically)
60. Stunde, die - hour
61. Supermarkt, der - supermarket
62. Tasche, die - purse, bag
63. (Tee) kochen - to boil, to brew
64. Toilette, die - bathroom
65. U-Bahn, die - metro, subway
66. über, (z.B. eine Stunde) lang - through, in (time)
67. ungefähr - roughly, approximately
68. unter - among
69. Vogel, der - bird
70. vom Anfang an - from the beginning
71. vorbei, neben - past, near
72. wachsen - to grow
73. weit - far (away), at a long distance
74. welcher - which

75. Wetter, der - weather
76. Wurst, die - baloney, kielbasa, sausage
77. zehn - ten
78. zu Fuß - on foot
79. Zucker, der - sugar
80. zurück - back
81. zwischen - between

B

Ich stehe um sieben Uhr morgens auf. Dann gehe ich ins Badezimmer. Ich wasche mein Gesicht und putze die Zähne. Es dauert fünf Minuten. Manchmal dusche ich mich auch am Morgen.

Dann gehe ich in die Küche. Ich trinke Kaffee am Morgen. Ich gieße Wasser in den Kessel und stelle ihn auf den Herd. Ich koche etwas Kaffee. Ich gieße den Kaffee in eine Tasse ein. Ich trinke Kaffee ohne Zucker. Dann nehme ich eine Schüssel. Ich schütte Cerealien in die Schüssel. Ich gebe etwas Milch hinzu. Ich füge noch einige Löffel Zucker oder Honig hinzu. Ich nehme einen Apfel und schneide ihn in die Schüssel mit Cerealien. Ich kann auch ein belegtes Brot machen. Ich Schneide ein Stück Brot und lege etwas Wurst und Käse darauf. Es dauert zwanzig Minuten.

Ich muss zur Universität gehen. Ich gehe in mein Zimmer. Ich sammle Bücher und Hefte in einer Tasche. Ich gehe nach draußen.

Das Wetter draußen ist gut. Ich gehe der Straße entlang. Um die Universität zu erreichen, muss ich O-Bus Nummer Sieben oder Neun nehmen. Ich kann dort auch mit Minibus Nummer Sieben oder Zehn fahren. Es ist nicht weit zur Haltestelle. Es dauert ungefähr fünf Minuten. Ich stehe an der Haltestelle. Es gibt viele Leute an der Haltestelle. Minibus Nummer Sieben kommt. Ich steige ein. Dann bezahle ich. Die Fahrt

I get up at seven o'clock in the morning. Then I go to the bathroom. In the bathroom, I wash my face and brush my teeth. It takes me five minutes. Sometimes in the morning I take a shower.

Then I go to the kitchen. In the morning I drink coffee. I pour the water into the teapot. I put the kettle on the stove. I brew some coffee. I pour the coffee into the cup. I drink coffee without sugar. Then I take a bowl. I pour cereal into the bowl. I add milk to it. I add several spoons of sugar or honey. I take an apple and I cut it into the bowl of cereal. I can also make a sandwich. I cut a piece of bread and put some sausage and cheese on the bread. It takes me twenty minutes.

I need to head to university. I go to my room. I gather books and notebooks into a bag. The bag is near the chair. I go outside.

The weather is good outside. I walk down the street. In order to get to university, I need trolleybus number seven or nine. I can also get there with minibus number seven or ten. It's not far to walk to the bus stop. It takes me about five minutes. I stand at the bus stop. There are a lot of people at the bus stop.

kostet drei Euro. Es gibt einen leeren Platz im Minibus. Ich setze mich. Ich steige nach fünf Haltestellen aus. Ich komme zur Universität. Es dauert ungefähr zwanzig Minuten.

Ich verlasse die Universität um drei Uhr. Ich gehe zurück zu Fuß. Ich gehe an einigen Läden vorbei. Ich gehe zwischen einem Museum und einem Theater. Dann gehe ich über eine Brücke. Die Brücke liegt oberhalb eines Sees. Ich gehe durch einen Park. Ich gehe zwischen den Bäumen im Park. Ein großer Vogel sitzt auf einem Baum. Ich gehe an einem Auto vorbei. Eine Katze sitzt unter dem Auto. Ich gehe an einem Supermarkt vorbei. Mein Haus liegt nicht weit. Es liegt hinter dem Supermarkt. Ich gehe zu meinem Haus. Neben meinem Haus gibt es viele Blumen. Ich gehe zur Tür. Ich mach die Tür auf und gehe hinein.

Minibus number seven pulls in. I get on the minibus. Then I pay the fare. The fare is three euros. There is a free seat in the minibus. I sit down. After five stops, I get off the minibus. I come to university. It takes me about twenty minutes.

I leave university at three o'clock. I go back on foot. I walk past some shops. I walk between a museum and a theater. Then I walk over a bridge. The bridge is located above a lake. I walk through a park. I walk among the trees in the park. A large bird sits in a tree. I walk past a car. A cat sits under the car. I walk past a supermarket. My house is not far. It is located behind the supermarket. I come up to my house. Near my house there are many flowers. I go to the door. I open the door and go inside.

Fragen und Antworten

- Wann stehst du auf?

- Ich stehe um sieben Uhr auf.

- Putzest du deine Zähne am Morgen?

- Ja, ich putze meine Zähne jeden Morgen.

- Duschst du dich am Morgen?

- Manchmal dusche ich mich am Morgen.

- Trinkst du Tee oder Kaffee am Morgen?

- In der Regel trinke ich Kaffee.

- Trinkst du Kaffee mit Zucker?

- Nein, ich trinke Kaffee ohne Zucker.

- Wie lange isst du das Frühstück?

Questions and Answers

- What time do you get up?

- I get up at seven in the morning.

- Do you brush your teeth in the morning?

- Yes, I brush my teeth every morning.

- Do you take a shower in the morning?

- Sometimes, I take a shower in the morning.

- Do you drink tea or coffee in the morning?

- I usually drink coffee.

- Do you drink coffee with sugar?

- Es dauert zwanzig Minuten.
- Fährst du zur Universität mit der U-Bahn?
- Nein, in der Regel fahre ich mit dem Bus.
- Hast du einen langen Weg zur Haltestelle?
- Nein, die Haltestelle ist nicht weit.
- Wieviel kostet eine Fahrt?
- Die Fahrt kostet drei Euro.
- Wie viele Haltestellen gibt es an deinem Weg?
- Ich steige an der fünften Haltestelle aus.
- Dauert die Fahrt es lange?
- Ich bin an der Universität nach ungefähr zwanzig Minuten.
- Kommst du auch mit dem Bus zurück?
- Nein, zurück gehe ich zu Fuß.
- Gehst du immer den Straßen entlang?
- Zuerst gehe ich der Straße entlang neben den Haltestellen und dann gehe ich durch den Park.
- Wo ist dein Haus?
- Es steht hinter dem Supermarkt.
- Gibt es Blumen neben deinem Haus?
- Ja, es gibt viele Blumen neben meinem Haus.

- No, I drink coffee without sugar.
- For how long do you eat breakfast?
- It takes me twenty minutes.
- Do you go to university by subway?
- No, I usually get there by bus.
- Is it a long walk to the stop?
- No, the bus stop is not far.
- How much is the bus fare?
- The fare costs three euros.
- How many stops are there on your way?
- I get off the bus at the fifth stop.
- Does it take you a long time?
- I arrive at the university after about twenty minutes.
- Do you go back by bus too?
- No, I go back on foot.
- Do you always walk on the streets?
- First, I walk down the street past the shops, and then walk through the park.
- Where is your house?
- It is located behind the supermarket.
- Do flowers grow near your house?
- There are many flowers near my house.

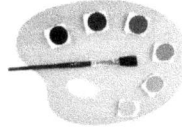

9

Ich gehe gerne ins Kino

I like going to the movies

A

Vokabeln

1. anfangen, beginnen - to start
2. aufwärmen - to warm (up)
3. Auto- - automobile (adj.)
4. (be)zahlen - to pay
5. bekommen, nach etwas greifen - to get, to reach, to take something out
6. besprechen - to discuss
7. bestellen - to order
8. Bus- - bus (adj.)
9. Bus, der - bus
10. dann - then, later
11. Dessert, das; der Nachtisch - cake, dessert
12. dreizehn - thirteen
13. dunkel - dark
14. Eis, das - ice cream

15. entgegen - towards
16. etwas - something
17. Fahrkarte, die - ticket
18. Film, der - film
19. Fluss, der - river
20. Freitag, der - Friday
21. Freundin, die - friend (female)
22. fünfzehn - fifteen
23. Hamburger, der - hamburger
24. Kasserolle, die; der (Koch)topf - saucepan
25. kaufen - to buy
26. Kellner, der - waiter
27. Komödie, die - comedy
28. lachen - to laugh
29. lecker - tasty
30. lustig - funny
31. Mikrowelle, die - microwave
32. Mittagsessen, das - lunch
33. reden, sich unterhalten - to talk
34. Sarah - Sarah
35. schnell - quickly
36. schrecklich, fürchterlich - scary
37. schütten - to pour (something loose)
38. schweigend - without speaking, silently
39. sich ankleiden - to get dressed
40. sich erwärmen - to warm up
41. sich verabschieden - to say goodbye
42. spazieren gehen - to take a walk
43. Spiel, das - game
44. Suppe, die - soup
45. süß - sweet
46. treffen - to meet
47. (über)kochen, sieden - to boil
48. Ufer, das - shore
49. Weg, der - path, way, road
50. weinen - to cry
51. weiter - further
52. zu Mittag essen - to have lunch
53. zusammen, gemeinsam - together

B

In der Regel komme ich nach Hause um drei Uhr. Ich gehe in mein Zimmer. Ich stelle meine Tasche auf den Tisch.

Ich gehe in die Toilette. Dann gehe ich ins Badezimmer. Ich wasche meine Hände und mein Gesicht. Manchmal nehme ich auch eine Dusche. Dann esse ich zu Mittag. In der Regel esse ich zu Mittag eine Suppe. Ich nehme einen

I usually come home at three o'clock. I go to my room. I put my bag on the table.

I go to the toilet. Then I go to the bathroom. I wash my hands and my face. Sometimes I might take a shower. Then I go have lunch. For lunch I usually eat soup. I take a pot of soup

Topf Suppe aus dem Kühlschrank. Ich stelle den Topf auf den Herd. Wenn die Suppe schon heiß ist, gieße ich sie in eine Schüssel für mich. Ich nehme einen Löffel und esse die Suppe. Ich esse auch Brot mit der Suppe. Ich gehe zum Küchenschrank. Ich nehme eine Messer aus dem Küchenschrank. Ich schneide einige Scheiben Brot. Manchmal esse ich Pizza. Meine Mutter macht eine gute Pizza. Ich schneide ein Stück Pizza ab. Dann wärme ich es in der Mikrowelle auf. Nach dem Mittagsessen esse ich noch etwas Süßes. Ich esse einen Kuchen. Das Kuchen ist lecker. Ich trinke auch Tee zum Kuchen. Ich stelle den Kessel auf dem Herd. Das Wasser kocht. Ich koche schwarzen Tee für mich. Ich schütte etwas Tee und zwei Löffel Zucker in die Tasse. Meine Katze kommt auch zum Mittagsessen. Ich gebe ihr etwas Milch. Nach dem Mittagsessen gehe ich mit dem Computer spielen. Der Computer ist in meinem Zimmer. Ich habe viele Computerspiele. Ich spiele ungefähr eine Stunde lang.

Ich gehe gerne ins Kino. Ich gehe mit meinen Freunden ins Kino jeden Freitag. Heute gehen wir auch. Der Film fängt in zwei Stunden an. Ich gehe ins Badezimmer, um eine Dusche zu nehmen. Dann gehe ich in mein Zimmer. Ich kleide mich an und gehe ins Kino. Ich verlasse das Haus. Es gibt ein rotes Auto neben dem Haus. Das ist das Auto meiner Mutter. Ich gehe der Straße entlang. Ich gehe an dem Supermarkt vorbei. Ich komme zur Haltestelle. Ich warte an der Haltestelle. Um ins Kino zu fahren, brauche ich Bus Nummer Dreizehn. Ich warte auf den Bus fünf Minuten lang. Bus Nummer Dreizehn kommt. Ich steige ein. Ich zahle für die Fahrkarte. Es gibt viele leere Plätze im Bus. Ich setze mich an das Fenster. Nach drei Haltestellen steige ich aus. Die Fahrt dauert ungefähr fünf Minuten. Ich gehe durch den Park. Es dauert zehn Minuten, das Kino zu erreichen. Auf dem Weg treffe ich meine

from the refrigerator. I put the pot on the stove. When the soup is hot, I pour it into a bowl for myself. I take a spoon and eat the soup. Along with the soup, I also eat bread. I go to the kitchen cabinet. Then I take a knife from the kitchen cabinet. I cut a few slices of bread. Sometimes, I eat pizza. My mom bakes good pizza. I slice a piece of pizza. Then I heat it in the microwave. After lunch, I can eat something sweet. I eat cake. The cake is delicious. I also drink tea with the cake. I put the kettle on the stove. The kettle boils. I brew black tea for myself. I pour some tea and two teaspoons of sugar into a cup. My cat also comes for dinner. I pour him some milk. I go to play on the computer after lunch. The computer is in my room. I have a lot of computer games. I play on the computer for an hour.

I like going to the movies. I go with my friends to the movies every Friday. Today we will go as well. The movie begins in two hours. I go to the bathroom to take a shower. Then I go to my room. I get dressed and go to the movies. I leave the house. There is a red car standing near our house. This is my mom's car. I walk down the street. I pass by the supermarket. I come up to the bus stop. I wait at the bus stop. To get to the theater, I need bus number thirteen. I wait for the bus for five minutes. Bus number thirteen pulls in. I get in the bus. I pay the fare. The bus has a lot of empty seats. I sit by the window. After three stops, I get off the bus. It takes me about fifteen minutes. I walk through the park. It takes ten minutes to get to the theater.

Freunde, Tom und Sarah.

Wir gehen ins Kino hinein. Ich kaufe Karten für eine sehr lustige Komödie. Wir gehen in den Saal und setzen uns auf unsere Plätze. Im Saal gibt es viele Leute. Wir lachen die ganze Zeit. Nach dem Film gehe ich mit Tom und Sarah in ein Café. Wir überqueren die Straße. Ein Mann mit einem Hund geht in unsere Richtung. Der Hund ist groß und fürchterlich. Wir gehen schnell weiter. Dann gehen wir an einem Museum vorbei. Dann gehen wir über die Brücke. Die Brücke befindet sich über dem Fluss. Wir sehen das Café neben dem Fluss. Es gibt nicht viele Leute im Café. Ein Kellner kommt zu uns. Sarah bestellt Eis. Tom und ich bestellen beide je einen Hamburger. Wir reden über den Film und lachen. Draußen ist es schon dunkel. Wir verlassen das Café. Wir müssen nach Hause gehen. Wir verabschieden uns. Sarah und Tom wohnen in der Nähe. Die gehen zu Fuß nach Hause. Ich gehe zur Bushaltestelle.

Along the way, I meet my friends Tom and Sarah.

We go inside the cinema. I buy tickets for a very funny comedy. We go into the hall and sit down in our seats. In the hall, there are a lot of people. We laugh the whole time. After the movie, Tom, Sarah and I and go to a cafe. We cross the road. A man with a dog comes towards us. The dog is big and scary. We pass quickly. Then we pass by a museum. Then we go over the bridge. The bridge is over the river. We see the cafe by the river. The cafe doesn't have many people. A waiter approaches us. Sarah orders ice cream. Tom and I each order a hamburger. We discuss the movie and laugh. It's already dark outside. We leave the cafe. We're going to go home. We say goodbye. Sarah and Tom live nearby. They go home on foot. I walk to the bus stop.

C

Fragen und Antworten

- Wann kommst du von der Universität zurück?

- Ich komme um drei Uhr nach Hause.

- Nimmst du eine Dusche, als du nach Hause kommst?

- Manchmal nehme ich eine Dusche.

- Was machst du später?

- Ich esse zu Mittag.

- Was isst du zu Mittag?

Questions and Answers

- What time do you come from university?

- I come at three o'clock.

- Do you take a shower when you come?

- I take a shower sometimes.

- What do you do then?

- Then I have lunch.

- What do you eat for lunch?

- I usually eat soup or pizza.

- In der Regel esse ich Suppe oder Pizza.
- Kochst du das Essen selbst?
- Nein, meine Mutter kocht es für mich.
- Trinkst du Tee nach dem Mittagsessen?
- Ja, ich trinke Tee zum Kuchen.
- Welchen Art Tee trinkst du?
- Ich mache schwarzen Tee für mich.
- Wieviel Zucker gibst du zum Tee?
- Ich gebe zwei Löffel Zucker.
- Was machst du später?
- Ich spiele mit dem Computer.
- Gehst du gerne ins Kino?
- Ja, ich gehe sehr gerne ins Kino.
- Gehst zu allein ins Kino?
- Nein, ich gehe mit meinen Freunden.
- Gehst du oft ins Kino?
- Ich gehe ins Kino jeden Freitag.
- Mit welchem Bus fährst du ins Kino?
- Ich fahre mit dem Bus Nummer Dreizehn.
- Nach wie vielen Haltestellen steigst du aus?
- Ich steige nach drei Haltestellen aus.
- Wie lang fährst du mit dem Bus?
- Es dauert ungefähr fünfzehn Minuten.
- Wie lange gehst du durch den Park zum Kino?
- Ich gehe durch den Park ungefähr zehn Minuten lang.
- Wen triffst du auf dem Weg?
- Ich treffe meine Freunde, Tom und Sarah.
- Wer kauft die Karten?

- Do you make the food yourself?
- No, my mother prepares it for me.
- Do you drink tea after lunch?
- Yes, I drink tea with cake.
- What kind of tea do you drink?
- I brew black tea for myself.
- How much sugar do you put in the tea?
- I put in two teaspoons of sugar.
- What do you do then?
- Then I play on the computer.
- Do you like going to the movies?
- Yes, I love going to the movies.
- Do you go to the movies alone?
- No, I go with my friends.
- Do you go to the movies often?
- I go to the movies every Friday.
- What bus do you take to the cinema?
- I go to the cinema on bus number thirteen.
- After how many stops do you get off the bus?
- I get off the bus after three stops.
- How long do you ride the bus?
- It takes me about fifteen minutes.
- For how long do you go through the park to the cinema?
- I walk through the park to the theater for ten minutes.
- Whom do you meet along the way?
- On the way, I meet my friends Tom and Sarah.

- Ich kaufe die Karten.

- Kaufst du Karten für eine Komödie oder für einen Kriminalfilm?

- Ich kaufe Karten für eine sehr lustige Komödie.

- Gibt es viele Leute im Saal?

- Es gibt viele Leute im Saal.

- Lacht ihr oder weint während des Filmes?

- Wir lachen die ganze Zeit.

- Gehst du nach Hause nach dem Film?

- Manchmal spaziere ich oder gehe in ein Café.

- Mit wem gehst du nach dem Film ins Café?

- Nach dem Film gehe ich mit Tom und Sarah ins Café.

- Wer geht in eure Richtung?

- Ein Mann mit einem Hund kommt in unsere Richtung.

- Wo ist das Café?

- Das Café liegt auf dem Ufer des Flusses.

- Was bestellt ihr?

- Sarah bestellt Eis und Tom und ich bestellen je einen Hamburger.

- Esst ihr in Stille oder redet ihr?

- Wir reden über den Film und lachen.

- Geht ihr danach gemeinsam nach Hause?

- Sarah und Tom gehen zu Fuß nach Hause. Ich gehe zur Haltestelle.

- Who buys the tickets?

- I buy the tickets.

- Do you buy tickets for a comedy or detective movie?

- I buy tickets for a very funny comedy.

- Are there a lot of people in the hall?

- There are a lot of people in the hall.

- During the movie, do you laugh or cry?

- We laugh the whole time.

- After the movie, do you go home?

- Sometimes I walk around or I go to a cafe.

- With whom do you go to the cafe after the movie?

- After the movie, Tom, Sarah and I and go to the cafe.

- Who comes towards you?

- A man with a dog comes towards us.

- Where is the cafe?

- The cafe is located on the bank of the river.

- What do you order?

- Sarah orders ice cream. Tom and I each order a hamburger.

- Do you eat in silence or do you talk?

- We discuss the movie and laugh.

- After the cafe, do you go home together?

- Sarah and Tom go home on foot. I walk to the bus stop.

10

Jack will Rechtsanwalt werden

Jack wants to be a lawyer

A

Vokabeln

1. absagen - to refuse
2. achthundert - eight hundred
3. Alkohol- - alcoholic
4. Ampel, die - traffic lights
5. Angaben, die - data, information
6. Arbeiter, der - worker
7. aufstehen - to wake up
8. ausfahren - to drive out
9. Ausgang, der - exit
10. Auskunfts- - information (adj.), referential (adj.)
11. aussehen - to look (like)
12. Autobahn, die - highway
13. bald - soon
14. Bank- - bank (adjective)
15. Bar, die; die Gaststätte - bar
16. Bargeld, das - cash
17. bekommen - to get (something)
18. brennen - to burn

19. Denkmal, das - memorial, monument
20. Ding, das - thing
21. Einpersonen- - single, with space for one person
22. Fahrer, der - driver
23. fliegen - to fly
24. Flug, der - flight
25. Flughafen, der - airport
26. Flugzeug, das - airplane
27. fotografieren - to take photos/pictures
28. fragen - to ask
29. führen, leiten - to lead, to drive
30. geben - to give
31. Geld, das - money
32. Gepäck, das - baggage
33. Getränk, das - drink
34. Hälfte, die - half
35. hinbringen - to bring, to carry
36. Hotel, das - hotel
37. irgendwann - sometime, some day
38. Kassierer, der - cashier, teller
39. kaufen - to buy
40. (Land)karte, die - map
41. Lebensmittelgeschäft, das - grocery (adj.)
42. lecker - tasty
43. nicht groß - not big
44. nicht teuer, preisgünstig - inexpensive
45. nie(mals) - never
46. nötig, notwendig - necessary
47. Parzelle, die - area, site
48. Pass, der - passport
49. Platz, der - (city) square
50. Polizist, der - policeman
51. (Rechts)anwalt, der - lawyer
52. Restaurant, das - restaurant
53. rufen - to call
54. (rund) um - around
55. sagen - to tell
56. Schlaf- - sleep (adj.)
57. Schlüssel, der - key
58. Springbrunnen, der; die Fontäne - fountain
59. Station, die; der Bahnhof - station
60. Stau, der - traffic jam
61. Taxi, das - taxi
62. Transport, der; der Verkehr - transport
63. Vorort, der; die Vorstadt - suburb
64. Wagen, der - wagon, carriage
65. warum - why
66. (weg)nehmen - to pick up, to take away
67. weitermachen - to continue
68. wohin - where to
69. Wohnung, die - apartment, flat
70. Wohnzimmer, das - living room
71. zeigen - to show
72. Zentrum, das - center
73. zustimmen - to agree

B

Heute kommt mein Freund Jack. Er soll mit dem Flugzeug kommen. Er soll um neun Uhr morgens auf dem Flughafen sein. Ich muss ihn dort treffen. Ich stehe auf, kleide mich an. Dann gehe ich in die Küche, um das Frühstück zu essen. Ich rufe ein Taxi. Das Taxi kommt in fünfzehn Minuten. Ich steige ein. Ich fahre zum Flughafen mit dem Taxi. Der Flughafen befindet sich im Vorort. Ich fahre durch die Stadt. In der Stadt gibt es Stau. Es dauert lang, durch die Stadt zu fahren. Dann verlasse ich die Stadt. Das Taxi fährt auf der Autobahn. Es dauert eine Stunde, den Flughafen zu erreichen. Ich fahre bis zum Flughafen. Dann bezahle ich dem Taxifahrer die Fahrt. Es ist acht Uhr dreißig. Jack kommt mit dem Flug Nummer Achthundertfünfzehn. Ich frage im Auskunftspunkt, wo der Ausgang für den Flug Achthundertfünfzehn ist. Ich warte auf Jacks Flugzeug. Das Flugzeug landet. Ich sehe Jack. Wir sammeln sein Gepäck ein. Neben dem Flughafen nehmen wir ein Taxi. Dann fahren wir ins Hotel. Jack wird im Hotel wohnen. Jack hat nicht so viel Geld. Ich kenne ein gutes und billiges Hotel. Es liegt in der Nähe meines Hauses. Wir fahren bis zum Hotel. Jack geht in die Richtung des Hotels. Er geht zur Rezeption. Jack will ein Einzelzimmer. Ein Hotelangestellte bittet Jack um seinen Pass. Der Hotelangestellte gibt seine Angaben in einen Computer ein. Jack zählt für sein Zimmer mit der Kreditkarte. Ein Hotelangestellter führt Jack zu seinem Zimmer und gibt ihm die Schlüssel. Sein Zimmer ist klein, aber gemütlich. Es gibt dort eine Küche, ein Bad, ein Wohnzimmer und ein Schlafzimmer.

Today my friend Jack is coming. He should arrive by plane. He will be at the airport at nine in the morning. I have to meet him there. I wake up, get dressed. Then I go to the kitchen for breakfast. I call a taxi. A taxi arrives in fifteen minutes. I get in the car. I go to the airport by taxi. The airport is located in the suburbs. I'm going through the city. There are traffic jams in the city. Driving takes a lot of time. Then I go out of the town. Taxi travels on a highway. It takes an hour to get to the airport. I drive up to the airport. Then I pay the fare to the taxi driver. It's eight thirty. Jack arrives on flight number eight hundred and fifteen. I ask at the information desk, where the exit for flight eight hundred and fifteen is. I'm waiting for Jack's plane. The plane lands. I see Jack. We pick up his luggage. We get in a taxi near the airport. Then we go to a hotel. Jack will stay at a hotel. Jack does not have a lot of money. I know a good and cheap hotel. It is close to my house. We drive up to the hotel. Jack approaches the hotel. He goes up to the hotel staff. Jack wants a single room. A hotel worker asks Jack to give his passport. Jack gives his passport. The desk clerk enters his data into a computer. Jack pays for the room by credit card. A hotel employee leads Jack to his room and gives him the keys. His room is small but cozy. It has a kitchen, bathroom, living room and bedroom.

Jack kam in die Stadt, um an der Universität zu studieren. Er will Rechtsanwalt werden. Jack bittet mich, ihm die Stadt zu zeigen. Ich stimme zu. Wir gehen auf die Straße. Das Wetter draußen ist gut. Wir gehen zur U-Bahn-Station. Jack ist noch nie mit der U-Bahn gefahren. Die Fahrkarte kostet zwei Euro. Wir steigen in den U-Bahn-Wagen ein. Wir fahren ins Zentrum. Die Fahrt dauert fünfundzwanzig Minuten. Im Stadtzentrum gibt es einen großen Platz und ein Denkmal. Das Denkmal ist groß und schön. Es gibt viele Leute rund um das Denkmal. Sie machen Fotos. Es gibt auch einen großen Springbrunnen. Viele Leute sitzen neben dem Springbrunnen. Wir gehen weiter. Ich zeige Jack Geschäfte. Dort kann man alles kaufen, was man braucht. Es gibt Lebensmittelgeschäfte, Kleidergeschäfte und andere Geschäfte. Dann führe ich Jack zur Universität. Wir gehen an dem Polizeirevier vorbei. Wir müssen über die Straße gehen Die Ampel ist rot. Wir warten. Die Ampel wird grün. Wir gehen über die Straße. Auf dem Weg zeige ich Jack Cafés und Restaurants, in denen man gut essen kann. Wir gehen neben einer Bar. Es gibt viele Alkoholgetränke in der Bar.	Jack came to the city to study at university. He wants to be a lawyer. Jack asks me to show him the city. I agree. We go out into the street. The weather is good outside. We go to the metro station. Jack has never ridden the subway. A metro ticket costs two euros. Then we get into a subway car. We are going to the city center. The ride there takes us twenty-five minutes. In the center of the city, there is a large square and a monument. The monument is big and beautiful. There are a lot of people around the monument. They are taking photos. There is also a large fountain. A lot of people seat near the fountain. We go farther. I show Jack shops. You can buy everything you need there. There are grocery stores, clothing stores and other shops. Then I lead Jack to his university. We pass by the police station. We need to cross the street. The traffic light is red. We wait. The light turns green. We cross the street. Along the way I show Jack cafes and restaurants where you can eat well. We pass by a bar. There are a lot of alcoholic beverages in the bar.

C

Fragen und Antworten	Questions and Answers
- Wer kommt heute?	- Who is coming today?
- Mein Freund Jack kommt heute.	- Today my friend Jack is arriving.
- Mit welcher Art Transport soll er kommen?	- What transport is he supposed to arrive on?
- Er soll mit dem Flugzeug kommen.	- He is supposed to come by airplane.

- Wann kommt er?	- At what time is he arriving?
- Er soll um neun Uhr morgens auf dem Flughafen sein.	- At nine in the morning he will be at the airport.
- Triffst du ihn dort?	- Are you going to meet him?
- Ja, ich muss ihn treffen.	- Yes, I have to meet him.
- Wohin gehst du, um zu frühstücken?	- Where do you go for breakfast?
- Ich gehe in die Küche, um dort Frühstück zu essen.	- I go to the kitchen for breakfast.
- Fährst du zum Flughafen mit dem Bus oder wirst du ein Taxi rufen?	- Will you go to the airport by bus or will you call a taxi?
- Ich rufe ein Taxi.	- I will call a taxi.
- Wie schnell kommt das Taxi?	- How soon does the taxi arrive?
- Das Taxi kommt in fünfzehn Minuten.	- The taxi arrives in fifteen minutes.
- Wo ist der Flughafen?	- Where is the airport?
- Der Flughafen befindet sich im Vorort.	- The airport is located in the suburbs.
- Gibt es Stau in der Stadt?	- Are there traffic jams in the city?
- Ja, es gibt Stau in der Stadt.	- Yes, there are traffic jams in the city.
- Wie lange dauert es, zum Flughafen zu fahren?	- How long does it take to get to the airport?
- Es dauert eine Stunde, zum Flughafen zu fahren.	- It takes an hour to get to the airport.
- Mit welchem Flug kommt Jack?	- Which flight does Jack arrive on?
- Jack kommt mit dem Flug Nummer Achthundertfünfzehn.	- Jack arrives on flight eight hundred and fifteen.
- Was fragst du am Auskunftspunkt?	- What do you ask at the help desk?
- Ich frage, wo sich der Ausgang für Flug Achthundertfünfzehn befindet.	- I ask at the help desk where the exit for flight eight hundred and fifteen will be.
- Was machst du auf dem Flughafen?	- What are you doing at the airport?
- Ich warte auf Jacks Flugzeug.	- I'm waiting for Jack's plane.
- Gehst du mit Jack zum Café?	- Do you and Jack go to a cafe?
- Nein, wir sammeln sein Gepäck ein.	- No, we pick up his luggage.
- Geht ihr zur Bushaltestelle?	- Do you go to a bus stop?

- Nein, wir gehen zum Taxi neben dem Flughafen.

- Wohin fahrt ihr?

- Wir fahren ins Hotel.

- Wird Jack in einem Hotel oder in einer Wohnung wohnen?

- Jack wird im Hotel wohnen.

- Hat Jack viel Geld?

- Nein, Jack hat nicht so viel Geld.

- Hilfst du Jack, ein billiges Hotel zu finden?

- Ja, ich kenne ein gutes und billiges Hotel.

- Kannst du sagen, wo es ist?

- Es ist in der Nähe meines Hauses.

- Fahrt ihr zu deinem Haus oder ins Hotel?

- Wir fahren zum Hotel.

- Wohin geht Jack?

- Jack geht in das Hotel hinein.

- Wem nähert sich Jack?

- Jack nähert sich an einen Hotelangestellten.

- Was für ein Zimmer will Jack?

- Jack will ein Einzelzimmer.

- Was fragt der Hotelangestellte Jack?

- Der Angestellte bittet Jack, ihm seinen Pass zu geben.

- Gibt ihm Jack seinen Pass?

- Ja, Jack gibt ihm seinen Pass.

- Wer gibt seine Angaben in den Computer ein?

- Der Hotelangestellte gibt seine Angaben in den Computer ein.

- Zählt Jack für das Zimmer mit dem

- No, we get in a taxi near the airport.

- Where are you going?

- We're going to a hotel.

- Will Jack stay in a hotel or an apartment?

- Jack will live at a hotel.

- Does Jack have a lot of money?

- No, Jack does not have a lot of money.

- Will you help Jack find a cheap hotel?

- Yes, I know a good and cheap hotel.

- Will you say where it is?

- It is near my house.

- Do you drive up to your house or the hotel?

- We drive up to the hotel.

- Where does Jack go?

- Jack enters the hotel.

- Whom does he approach?

- He approaches a hotel employee.

- What kind of room does Jack want?

- Jack wants a single room.

- What does the hotel worker ask Jack?

- The employee of the hotel asks Jack to give his passport.

- Does Jack give his passport?

- Yes, Jack gives his passport.

- Who puts his data into the computer?

- The desk clerk enters his data into a computer.

Bargeld?

- Nein, Jack zählt für das Zimmer mit der Kreditkarte.

- Bekommt Jack seine Schlüssel vom Hotelangestellten und geht er dann ins Zimmer?

- Nein, der Hotelangestellte führt Jack zu seinem Zimmer und gibt ihm die Schlüssel.

- Ist sein Zimmer groß oder klein?

- Sein Zimmer ist klein aber gemütlich.

- Gibt es eine Küche in seinem Zimmer?

- Ja, es gibt eine Küche, ein Bad, ein Wohnzimmer und ein Schlafzimmer.

- Warum kommt Jack in die Stadt?

- Jack kommt in die Stadt, um an der Universität zu studieren.

- Wer will er werden?

- Er will Rechtsanwalt werden.

- Warum bittet dich Jack?

- Jack bittet mich, ihm die Stadt zu zeigen.

- Stimmst du zu oder verweigerst du es?

- Ich stimme zu.

- Wohin geht ihr?

- Wir gehen nach draußen.

- Wie ist das Wetter draußen?

- Draußen ist das Wetter gut.

- Wohin geht ihr?

- Wir gehen zur U-Bahn-Station.

- Ist Jack schon mit der U-Bahn gefahren?

- Jack ist noch nie mit der U-Bahn gefahren.

- Wieviel kostet die Fahrkarte?

- Does Jack pay for the room in cash?

- No, Jack pays for the room by credit card.

- Does Jack receive the keys from the cashier and then go into the room?

- No, the hotel worker leads Jack to his room and gives him the keys.

- Is his room is big or small?

- His room is small but cozy.

- Is there a kitchen in his room?

- Yes, it has a kitchen, bathroom, living room and bedroom.

- Why did Jack come to the city?

- Jack came to the city to study at university.

- What does he want to become?

- He wants to become a lawyer.

- What does Jack ask you for?

- Jack asks me to show him the city.

- Do you agree or refuse?

- I agree.

- Where do you go?

- We go outside.

- What's the weather like outside?

- Outside the weather is good.

- Where do you go?

- We go to the subway station.

- Has Jack ever ridden a subway?

- Jack has never ridden a subway.

- How much is the fare on the subway?

- The subway fare costs two euros.

- Where are you going?

- Die Fahrkarte kostet zwei Euro.
- Wohin fahrt ihr?
- Wir fahren ins Zentrum.
- Wie lange dauert die Fahrt?
- Die Fahrt dauert fünfundzwanzig Minuten.
- Was gibt es im Zentrum?
- Im Zentrum gibt es einen großen Platz und ein Denkmal.
- Wie sieht das Denkmal aus?
- Das Denkmal ist groß und schön.
- Wie viele Leute gibt es rund um das Denkmal?
- Es gibt viele Leute rund um das Denkmal.
- Was machen sie?
- Sie machen Fotos.
- Was gibt es dort noch?
- Es gibt einen großen Springbrunnen.
- Gibt es viele Leute am Springbrunnen?
- Viele Leute sitzen am Springbrunnen.
- Was zeigst du Jack noch?
- Ich zeige ihm Geschäfte.
- Kann man dort alle nötigen Dinge kaufen?
- Man kann dort alles kaufen, was man braucht.
- Welche Geschäfte sind es?
- Es sind Lebensmittelgeschäfte, Kleidergeschäfte und andere.
- Wohin führst du Jack?
- Ich führe Jack zu seiner Universität.
- An welchem Gebäuden gehr ihr vorbei?

- We're going to the city center.
- How much time does the ride there take?
- The ride there takes us twenty-five minutes.
- What is in the city center?
- There is a large square and a monument in the center.
- What is the monument like?
- The monument is big and beautiful.
- How many people are there around the monument?
- There are a lot of people around the monument.
- What are they doing?
- They are taking pictures.
- What else is there?
- There is also a large fountain.
- Are there many or few people at the fountain?
- A lot of people are sitting at the fountain.
- What else do you show Jack?
- I show Jack shops.
- Can you buy all necessary things there?
- You can buy everything you need there.
- What kind of shops are there?
- There are grocery stores, clothing stores and other shops.
- Where do you lead Jack?
- I lead Jack to his university.
- What kind of building do you go past?
- We go past a police station.

- Wir gehen an einem Polizeirevier vorbei.
- Musst ihr über die Straße gehen?
- Ja, wir müssen über die Straße gehen.
- Welche Farbe hat die Ampel?
- Die Ampel ist rot.
- Geht ihr bei dem roten Licht oder wartet ihr auf das grüne Licht?
- Wir warten, bis die Ampel grün wird.
- Geht ihr über die Straße oder bleibt ihr stehen?
- Wir gehen über die Straße.
- Zeigst du Jack, wo man essen kann?
- Ja, auf dem Weg zeige ich Jack Cafés und Restaurants, in denen man essen kann.
- An welchem Ort geht ihr vorbei?
- Wir gehen an einer Bar vorbei.
- Gibt es viele Alkoholgetränke in der Bar?
- Ja, es gibt viele Alkoholgetränke in der Bar.

- Do you need to cross the road?
- Yes, we need to cross the road.
- What kind of light is lit at the traffic lights?
- There is a red light at the traffic lights.
- Do you walk on a red light or wait for a green light?
- We are waiting for the green light to light up.
- Do you cross the road or continue to stand?
- We cross the road.
- Do you show Jack where you can eat?
- Yes, on the way, I show Jack cafes and restaurants where you can eat.
- What kind of place do you pass?
- We pass a bar.
- Are there many or few alcoholic beverages in the bar?
- There are a lot alcoholic beverages in the bar.

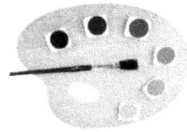

11

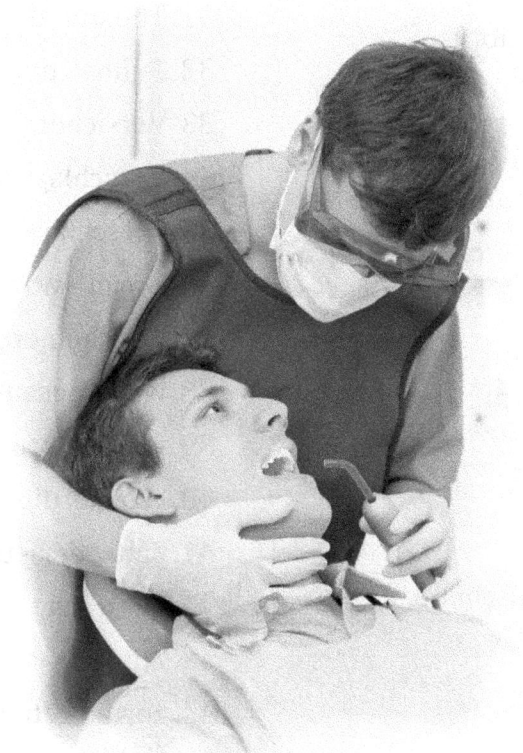

Jack ist krank

Jack is sick

A

Vokabeln

1. Anstellung, die; die Beschäftigung - employment, job
2. Apotheke, die - drugstore
3. behandelt werden - to get treated
4. Behandlung, die - treatment
5. Berater, der - consultant
6. Berg, der - hill, mountain
7. besser - better
8. Bibliothek, die; die Bücherei - library
9. deshalb - so, because of this

10. Erde, die; der Boden - earth, ground, soil
11. fühlen - to feel
12. genug sein; greifen - to be enough; to grab
13. Grünfläche, die - greenery
14. hier(her) - here (direction)
15. Klinik, die - clinic
16. krank sein - to be sick
17. Lebensmittel, die - products, food
18. -mal (einmal, zweimal etc.) - time(s) (as in "how many times")
19. neunzehn - nineteen
20. Preis, der; die Kosten (pl.) - value, price
21. Schüler, der - student, pupil
22. schwimmen - to swim
23. (Selbstbedienungs)Wäscherei, die - laundromat, launderette
24. sich bewegen - to move
25. Strand, der - beach
26. Student, der - university student
27. suchen - to search, to look for
28. Tag, der - day
29. Technologie, die - technology
30. teuer - expensive
31. Theater, das - theater
32. Tunnel, der - tunnel
33. Versicherung, die - insurance
34. Vorschlag, der - suggestion
35. vorschlagen - to suggest, to offer
36. warm - warm
37. waschen - to wash, launder
38. weil - because
39. werden - to become
40. Woche, die - week
41. Zahn, der - tooth
42. Zahnarzt, der - dentist
43. Zug, der - train
44. zurückgeben, abgeben - to give in, return

B

Jack ist Student. Er ist neunzehn Jahre alt. Er studiert an der Universität für Technologie und Design. Er kann zur Universität mit der U-Bahn oder mit dem Bus kommen. In der Regel wählt er die U-Bahn. Die Fahrkarte kostet zwei Euro. Die Fahrt dauert ungefähr zwanzig Minuten. Der Zug fährt zuerst unter der Erde, dann überquert er den Fluss über eine Brücke.

Jack is a college student. He is nineteen. He is studying at the University of Technology and Design. He can get to the university by bus or subway. Jack usually goes by subway. The fare is two euros. He rides the subway for about twenty minutes. The subway train moves underground at first, and afterwards, it goes on the bridge over the river.

In der Regel macht Jack sein Essen nicht selbst. In unserer Stadt sind Restaurants teuer, deshalb isst Jack normalerweise in einem Café. Er geht auch in den Supermarkt, um Lebensmittel zu kaufen.

Jack geht in die Selbstbedienungswäscherei, um seine Kleidung zu waschen. Jack hat keine Waschmaschine in seinem Zimmer. Er gibt schmutzige Kleidung in der Wäscherei ab.

Jack mag die Stadt. Er wollte immer in einer Großstadt wohnen. Die Stadt ist schön. Sie liegt am Ufer eines Flusses. Die Stadt hat viele interessanten Orte. Viele Touristen kommen hierher.

Jack ist krank. Er hat Zahnschmerzen. Er geht in die Klinik. Jack geht zum Zahnarzt. Er hat eine Versicherung, deshalb bezahlt er nur die Hälfte der Kosten. Nach der Behandlung fühlt sich Jack besser. Er geht zur Universität und fühlt sich gut.

Jack spaziert oft durch die Stadt. Er geht in den Park. Er mag es, dass es in der Stadt viele Grünflächen gibt. Die Stadt ist sauber. Das Wetter ist warm. Manchmal geht Jack zum Strand am Fluss. Er schwimmt gut. Er geht auch ins Kino, zu Museen und in den Theater mit seinen Freunden. Jack mag diese Stadt. Er mag es auch zu lesen. Jede Woche geht er in die Bibliothek. Er mag Kriminalromane. Er liest jeden Tag durch.

Jack hat nicht genug Geld. Er will eine Anstellung finden. Er geht zum Arbeitsamt. Er will dreimal pro Woche arbeiten. Er bekommt einen Vorschlag, als Berater in einem Supermarkt zu arbeiten. Jack nimmt die Arbeit an.

Jack usually does not prepare food himself. In our city restaurants are expensive, so Jack usually eats in a cafe. He also goes to the supermarket to buy food.

Jack goes to the laundromat to wash his clothes. Jack has no washing machine in his room. He gives dirty clothes to the laundromat.

Jack likes this city. He always wanted to live in a big city. The city is beautiful. It is located on the banks of the river. The city has many places of interest. A lot of tourists come here.

Jack is sick. He has a toothache. He goes to the clinic. Jack goes to the dentist. He has insurance, so he pays half the cost of treatment. After the treatment, Jack gets better. He goes to university and feels good.

Jack walks around the city often. He walks to the park. He likes that there is a lot of greenery in this city. The city is clean. The weather is warm. Jack sometimes goes to the beach at the river. He swims well. He also goes to the movies, museums and theaters with his friends. Jack likes this city. Jack also likes to read. Every week he goes to the library. He likes detective stories. He reads books every day.

Jack does not have enough money. He wants to find a job. He goes to the employment center. He wants to work three times a week. He is offered a job as a supermarket consultant. Jack agrees.

C

Fragen und Antworten	**Questions and Answers**

- Ist Jack ein Schüler oder ein Student?
- Er ist Student.
- Wie alt ist er?
- Er ist neunzehn Jahre alt.
- Wo studiert er?
- Er studiert an der Universität für Technologie und Design.
- Wie kommt er zur Universität?
- Er kann mit dem Bus oder mit der U-Bahn zur Universität fahren. In der Regel fährt er mit der U-Bahn.
- Wieviel kostet eine Fahrkarte für die U-Bahn?
- Die Karte kostet zwei Euro.
- Wie lang fährt er mit der U-Bahn?
- Die Fahrt dauert ungefähr zwanzig Minuten.
- Fährt der Zug die ganze Zeit durch den Tunnel?
- Er fährt zuerst unter der Erde, dann überquert er den Fluss über eine Brücke.
- Kocht sich Jack das Essen selbst?
- Nein, in der Regel macht er das Essen nicht selbst.
- Wo isst Jack in der Regel?
- In der Regel isst Jack in einem Café.
- Warum isst Jack nicht in einem Restaurant?
- Weil Restaurants in unserer Stadt teuer

- Is Jack a high school or college student?
- Jack is a college student.
- How old is he?
- He is nineteen years old.
- Where does he study?
- He studies at the University of Technology and Design.
- How does he get to the university?
- He can get to the university by bus or subway. Jack usually goes by subway.
- What is the cost of travel on the subway?
- The fare is two euros.
- For how long does he ride on the subway?
- He rides the subway for about twenty minutes.
- Does the subway train ride the whole time in the tunnel underground?
- The subway train moves at first underground, then across the bridge over the river.
- Does Jack cook food for himself?
- No, Jack usually does not prepare food himself.
- Where does Jack usually eat?
- Jack usually eats in a café.
- Why does Jack not eat in a restaurant?
- Because in our city restaurants are

sind.

- Kauft Jack auch Lebensmittel in einem Supermarkt?

- Ja, er geht auch in den Supermarkt, um Lebensmittel zu kaufen.

- Wo wäscht Jack seine Kleidung?

- Jack wäscht seine Kleidung in der Selbstbedienungswäscherei.

- Mag Jack die Stadt?

- Ja, Jack wollte immer in einer Großstadt wohnen.

- Liegt die Stadt im Gebirge oder an einem Fluss?

- Die Stadt liegt am Ufer eines Flusses.

- Gibt es Touristen in der Stadt?

- Ja, es gibt viele Touristen hier.

- Warum ist Jack krank?

- Er hat Zahnschmerzen.

- Geht er in die Apotheke oder in die Klinik?

- Er geht in die Klinik. Er geht zu einem Arzt.

- Zu welchem Arzt geht Jack?

- Jack geht zu einem Zahnarzt.

- Kostet die Behandlung beim Zahnarzt viel?

- Jack hat eine Versicherung, deshalb bezahlt er nur die Hälfte der Kosten.

- Wie fühlt sich Jack nach der Behandlung?

- Jack fühlt sich besser. Er fährt zur Universität und fühlt sich besser.

- Mag es Jack, durch die Stadt zu spazieren?

- Ja, Jack spaziert sehr oft durch die Stadt.

- Wohin geht Jack?

- Jack geht in den Park. Er mag es, dass es in

expensive.

- Does he buy food at the supermarket?

- Yes, he also goes to the supermarket to buy food.

- Where does Jack wash his clothes?

- Jack washes his clothes in the laundromat.

- Does Jack like this city?

- Yes, Jack always wanted to live in a big city.

- Is the city located in the mountains or by the river?

- The city is located on the banks of the river.

- Are there tourists in the city?

- Yes, a lot of tourists come here.

- Why is Jack sick?

- He has a toothache.

- Does he go to the pharmacy or clinic?

- He goes to the clinic. Jack goes to the doctor.

- Which doctor does Jack go to?

- Jack goes to the dentist.

- Is it expensive for Jack to be treated by the dentist?

- He has insurance, so he pays half the cost of treatment.

- How does Jack feel after the treatment?

- Jack gets better. He goes to university and feels good.

- Does Jack like to walk around the city?

- Yes, Jack walks around the city often.

der Stadt viele Grünflächen gibt.

- Kann Jack schwimmen?

- Ja, Jack schwimmt gut. Manchmal geht er zum Strand am Fluss.

- Wohin geht Jack mit seinen Freunden?

- Er geht ins Kino, zu Museen und in das Theater.

- Wie oft geht Jack in die Bibliothek?

- Jack geht jede Woche in die Bibliothek.

- Welche Bücher mag er?

- Er mag Kriminalromane. Er liest jeden Tag Bücher.

- Hat Jack viel Geld?

- Nein, er hat nicht genug Geld.

- Wo sucht Jack eine Arbeit?

- Er geht zum Arbeitsamt.

- Wie viele Tage pro Woche kann Jack arbeiten?

- Er will dreimal pro Woche arbeiten.

- Was für einen Arbeitsvorschlag bekommt er?

- Er bekommt einen Vorschlag, als Berater im Supermarkt zu arbeiten.

- Nimmt er den Vorschlag an oder lehnt er ihn ab?

- Er nimmt den Vorschlag an.

- Where does Jack walk?

- He walks in the park. He likes that in this city there is a lot of greenery.

- Does Jack swim?

- Yes, Jack swims well. He sometimes goes to the beach at the river.

- Where does Jack go with his friends?

- He goes to the movies, museums and theaters.

- How often does Jack go to the library?

- Jack goes to the library every week.

- What kind of books does he like?

- He likes detective stories. He reads books every day.

- Does Jack have a lot of money?

- No, Jack does not have enough money.

- Where does Jack look for a job?

- He goes to the employment center.

- How many days a week can Jack work?

- He wants to work three times a week.

- What kind of job he is offered?

- He was offered a job as a supermarket consultant.

- Does Jack accept the offer or refuse?

- Jack agrees.

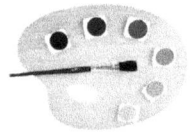

12

Jack will eine neue Wohnung finden

Jack wants to find a new apartment

 A

Vokabeln

1. ablehnen - to refuse
2. Addresse, die - address
3. angezeigt - indicated
4. antworten - to answer
5. Anzeige, die - announcement, ad
6. anzeigen, andeuten - to indicate
7. Aufzug, der - elevator
8. Bank, die - bank
9. begleiten; verbringen - to accompany; to spend (time)
10. Bett, das - bed
11. Buch- - book (adj.)
12. Bürgersteig, der; der Fußweg - sidewalk
13. denken - to think
14. draußen - outside

15. dreihundert - three hundred
16. dritter - third
17. einen Vertrag schließen - enter into a contract
18. einladen - to invite
19. entlang - along
20. entscheiden - to decide
21. Entschluss, der; die Entscheidung - decision
22. erklären - to explain
23. erster - first
24. Etage, die - floor, storey
25. finden - to find
26. geeignet, passend - suitable, fitting
27. gemütlich - cozily
28. hell - bright
29. herangehen, sich nähern - to approach
30. hoch - high
31. innen, drinnen - inside
32. jemand - someone
33. jene(r/s) - that
34. Kind, das - child
35. Kiosk, der - kiosk
36. Klingel, die - bell, ring
37. klopfen - to knock
38. lange - long, for a long time
39. Laptop, der - laptop
40. laut - noisily / noisy
41. ledern, Leder- - leather (adj.)
42. Möbel, die - furniture
43. Monat, der - month
44. nicht groß - not tall
45. Periode, die - period
46. Preis, der - price
47. Richtung, die - direction
48. ruhig - calm(ly)
49. sagen - to tell
50. Samstag, der - Saturday
51. sich verabreden - to arrange, to make an appointment
52. so - like this, so
53. sofort, auf der Stelle - right away
54. steigen - to go up, to ascend, to rise
55. still - quiet
56. still, leise - quietly
57. treffen - to meet
58. Treppenhaus, das - staircase
59. umziehen - to move (to change address)
60. Unterkunft, die; die Wohnung - accomodation, apartment
61. Vertreter, der; der Agent - agent
62. wählen - to choose
63. Wirt, der - owner
64. Zeitung, die - newspaper
65. zentral - central
66. zurückkehren - to return
67. zweiter - second

B

Heute ist Samstag. Es ist teuer, lange in einem Hotel zu bleiben. Jack will eine neue Wohnung finden. Er kauft eine Zeitung am Kiosk. In der Zeitung gibt es viele Anzeigen. Jack geht in ein Café und setzt sich an einen Tisch. Er bestellt Kaffee. Er sitzt im Café und liest die Zeitung. Er findet einige passenden Wohnungen in der Zeitung. Ihre Preise sind niedrig. Jack will auch, dass sich die Wohnung in der Nähe der Universität befindet. Er wählt drei Wohnungen. Jack will sie noch heute sehen. Er ruft die Telefonnummer an, die in den Anzeigen angegeben sind. Die erste Nummer antwortet nicht. Dann ruft er die zweite Nummer. Eine Frau antwortet. Sie heißt Charlotte. Sie ist eine Immobilienagentin. Er verabredet sich mit ihr. Jack findet es gut, dass die Wohnung sich im Zentrum der Stadt befindet. Er steigt in einen Bus ein und fährt zu diesem Haus. Als Jack ankommt, sieht er ein hohes Haus. Es befindet sich am Zentralplatz. Es gibt viele Leute und Autos. Jack findet es nicht gut, dass es hier so laut ist. Das Haus gefällt ihm auch von außen nicht so gut. Es sieht alt aus. Jack geht hinein. Die Wohnung befindet sich in der zweiten Etage. Er klopft an die Tür. Eine Frau öffnet die Tür. Das ist Charlotte. Sie lädt Jack ein, sich die Wohnung anzusehen. Er kommt hinein. Die Wohnung ist geräumig, aber alt. Es gibt große Fenster. Sie sind hölzern. Im Wohnzimmer gibt es einen großen Fernseher und ein Sofa. Jack geht in das Schlafzimmer hinein. Es hat ein großes Bett. In der Ecke des Zimmers gibt es einen Tisch. Jack mag es nicht, dass die Wohnung dunkel ist und wenige Möbel hat. Sie sieht leer aus. Jack sagt Charlotte, dass er heute

Today is Saturday. Living in a hotel for a long time is expensive. Jack wants to find an apartment to live in. He buys a newspaper at a kiosk. There are many ads in the newspaper. Jack walks into a cafe and sits down at a table. He orders some coffee. He is sitting in a cafe and looks at the newspaper. He finds a few suitable apartments in the newspaper. Their prices are low. Jack also wants the apartment to be near his university. He chooses three apartments for himself. Jack wants to see them today. He calls the phone numbers listed in the ads. The first number does not answer. Then he calls another number. A woman responds. Her name is Charlotte. She is a real estate agent. He arranges to meet her. Jack likes it that the house is in the center of the city. He gets on the bus and goes to the house. When Jack arrives, he sees a tall house. It is located in the central square. There are a lot of cars and people. Jack did not like the fact that it is so noisy there. He also did not like the house from the outside. It looks old. Jack enters the house. The apartment is on the second floor. He knocks on the door. A woman opens the door. It is Charlotte. She invites Jack to see the apartment. He comes in. The apartment is spacious, but old. There are large windows. They are wooden. The living room has a large TV and a sofa. Jack goes into the bedroom. It has a large bed. In the corner of the room there is a table. Jack did not like the fact that the apartment is dark and has little furniture. It looks empty. Jack tells Charlotte that wants to see another apartment today

noch eine Wohnung ansehen will und dann entscheiden. Charlotte bittet ihn, am Abend anzurufen und ihr die Entscheidung mitzuteilen. Jack verlässt das Haus. Er ruft noch eine Nummer an. Ein Mann vermietet eine Wohnung in der Nähe. Er heißt Mike. Er erklärt, wie man sein Haus findet. Jack kennt dieses Ort. Er geht zur U-Bahn-Station. Die Wohnung befindet sich neben einem Park. Jack steigt in den Wagen ein. Die Fahrt dauert ungefähr zehn Minuten. Er geht draußen und dann auf den Bürgersteig dem Weg entlang. Er kann das Haus nicht finden, aber er hat die Adresse. Er geht zu einer Frau mit einem Kind. Er fragt, wie man das Haus finden kann. Die Frau kennt das Haus. Sie wohnt dort. Sie zeigt Jack die Richtung, die er wählen soll. Das Haus befindet sich neben einer Bank. Jack geht hinein. Es gefällt ihm sehr, dass sich das Haus neben einem Park befindet. Es ist still und ruhig rund um das Haus. Neben dem Haus gibt es einen Garten. Es gibt dort viele Blumen. Mikes Wohnung ist in der dritten Etage. Jack geht zum Aufzug. Er fährt auf die dritte Etage. Jack geht aus dem Aufzug hinaus. Er benutzt die Klingel. Ein Mann öffnet die Tür. Das ist Mike. Er begleitet Jack in die Wohnung.

Drinnen ist es hell und bequem. Es gibt neue Möbel in der Wohnung. Im Zimmer gibt es einen Großbildfernseher. Er ist neu. In der Zimmerecke gibt ein Bett. Im Zimmer sieht Jack ein Bücherregal. Es gibt viele Bücher im Bücherregal. In der Mitte des Zimmers gibt es einen Tisch. Neben dem Tisch gibt es einen Sessel. Er ist ledern. Jack denkt daran, seinen Laptop dorthin zu stellen. Das Haus gefällt ihm. Er sagt Mike, dass er hier wohnen will. Er soll Mike dreihundert Euro pro Monat bezahlen. Sie schließen einen Vertrag. Jack muss für zwei Monaten sofort bezahlen. Er bringt am selben Tag alle

and decide. Charlotte asks Jack to call in the evening and announce his decision. Jack leaves the house. He calls one more number. A man rents out an apartment nearby. The man's name is Mike. He explains how to get to the house. Jack knows this place. He goes to the subway station. This apartment is located near a park. Jack goes into a subway car. He rides the subway for about ten minutes. He gets out of the subway and walks on the sidewalk along the road. He cannot find the house, but he has the address. He goes to a woman with a child. He asks her how to get to the house. The woman knows this house. She lives there. She points out to Jack the direction in which to go. The house is located near the bank. Jack comes to the house. He really likes that the house is located next to the park. It is quiet and peaceful around the house. Near the house, there is a garden. There are many flowers there. Mike's apartment is on the third floor. Jack goes into the elevator. He goes to the third floor. Jack comes out of the elevator. He rings the bell. A man opens the door. This is Mike. He accompanies Jack inside.

It is bright and comfortable inside. There is new furniture in the apartment. The room has a large-screen TV. It is new. In the corner of the room, there is a bed. Jack sees a bookshelf in the room. There are a lot of books in the bookshelf. In the middle of the room, there is a table. There is a big armchair next to the table. It's made of leather. Jack thinks about putting his laptop there. He likes the house. He tells Mike that he wants to live in this house. He will pay Mike three hundred euros per month. They enter into a contract. Jack has to pay for two months

seinen Sachen aus dem Hotel.

straight. He carries all his belongings out of the hotel on the same day.

C

Fragen und Antworten

- Was für ein Tag ist heute?

- Es ist Samstag.

- Warum will Jack eine Wohnung finden?

- Weil es teuer ist, eine lange Zeit im Hotel zu bleiben.

- Was kauft Jack am Kiosk?

- Am Kiosk kauft Jack eine Zeitung mit Anzeigen.

- Geht Jack zurück zum Hotel oder in ein Café?

- Jack geht in ein Café und setzt sich an den Tisch.

- Bestellt er Eis oder Kaffee?

- Er bestellt Kaffee.

- Was macht Jack im Café?

- Er sitzt und liest die Zeitung.

- Findet er Anzeigen für billige Wohnungen?

- Ja, er findet Anzeigen für einige passenden Wohnungen in der Zeitung.

- Wo soll sich die Wohnung befinden?

- Jack will eine Wohnung in der Nähe seiner Universität finden.

- Wählt Jack eine Wohnung?

- Ja, er wählt drei Wohnungen und will sie

Questions and Answers

- What day is it today?

- Today is Saturday.

- Why does Jack want to find an apartment to live in?

- Because living in a hotel for a long time is expensive.

- What does Jack buy at a kiosk?

- At a kiosk, Jack buys a newspaper with classified ads.

- Does Jack return to the hotel, or go to a cafe?

- Jack walks into a cafe and sits down at the table.

- Does he order an ice cream or coffee?

- He orders some coffee.

- What does Jack do in the cafe?

- He's sitting and reading the newspaper.

- Does he find ads for inexpensive apartments?

- Yes, he finds ads for a few suitable apartments in the newspaper.

- Where must the apartment be?

- Jack wants the apartment to be near his university.

- Does Jack choose an apartment?

- Yes, he chooses three apartments and

heute ansehen.

- Mit wem verabredet sich Jack?

- Mit einer Immobilienagentin. Sie heißt Charlotte.

- Warum wählt Jack diese Wohnung?

- Es gefällt ihm, dass sich die Wohnung im Stadtzentrum befindet.

- Kommt Jack zu diesem Haus zu Fuß oder mit dem Bus?

- Jack steigt in den Bus ein und fährt zu diesem Haus.

- Wo ist das Haus?

- Es befindet sich am Zentralplatz.

- Liegt das Haus in einem ruhigen oder lauten Ort?

- Es gibt viele Autos und Leute. Jack mag es nicht, dass es hier so laut ist.

- Gefiel ihm das Haus?

- Nein, von außen gefällt ihm das Haus nicht. Es sieht alt aus.

- In welcher Etage liegt die Wohnung?

- Die Wohnung liegt in der zweiten Etage.

- Wer öffnet die Tür?

- Charlotte öffnet die Tür.

- Ist die Wohnung neu oder alt?

- Die Wohnung ist geräumig, aber alt.

- Sind die Fenster in der Wohnung klein oder groß?

- Die Fenster sind groß. Sie sind hölzern.

- Was gibt es im Wohnzimmer?

- Das Wohnzimmer hat einen großen Fernseher und ein Sofa.

wants to see them today.

- With whom does Jack arrange to meet?

- A real estate agent. Her name is Charlotte.

- Why does Jack choose this house?

- Jack likes it that the house is in the center of the city.

- Does Jack go to the house on foot or by bus?

- Jack gets on the bus and rides to the house.

- Where is the house?

- It is located in the central square.

- Is the house located in a quiet or noisy place?

- There are a lot of cars and people. Jack does not like the fact that it is so noisy there.

- Did Jack like the house?

- No, he does not like the house from the outside. It looks old.

- On what floor is the apartment?

- The apartment is on the second floor.

- Who opens the door?

- Charlotte opens the door.

- Is the apartment new or old?

- The apartment is spacious, but old.

- Are the windows in the apartment small or large?

- The windows are large. They are wooden.

- What is there in the living room?

- The living room has a large TV and a sofa.

- Ist das Bett im Schlafzimmer groß?

- Ja, das Schlafzimmer hat ein großes Bett.

- Gibt es einen Tisch im Zimmer?

- Ja, ein Tisch ist in der Ecke.

- Gefällt Jack die Wohnung?

- Nicht sehr. Die Wohnung ist dunkel und es gibt wenige Möbel.

- Lehnt Jack die Wohnung ab?

- Nein, er sagt Charlotte, dass er noch eine Wohnung heute ansehen will und sich dann entschließen.

- Besucht Jack noch andere Wohnungen?

- Ja, er ruft noch eine Nummer an.

- Wie heißt der Vermieter?

- Er heißt Mike.

- Weiß Jack, wie man zu diesem Haus fährt?

- Ja, er geht zu einer U-Bahn-Station. Die Wohnung befindet sich in der Nähe eines Parks.

- Wie lange fährt Jack mit der U-Bahn?

- Er fährt mit der U-Bahn ungefähr zehn Minuten lang.

- Findet er das Haus sofort?

- Nein, er kann das Haus nicht finden, aber er hat die Adresse.

- Kann er jemanden fragen?

- Ja, er fragt eine Frau mit einem Kind.

- Wonach fragt Jack die Frau?

- Er fragt, wie man das Haus finden kann.

- Kennt die Frau dieses Haus?

- Ja, sie wohnt dort. Sie zeigt Jack die

- Is the bed in the bedroom big?

- Yes, the bedroom has a large bed.

- Is there a table in the room?

- The table is in the corner of the room.

- Does Jack like the apartment?

- No, not much. The apartment is dark and there is little furniture.

- Does Jack reject this apartment?

- No, he tells Charlotte that he wants to see another apartment today and decide.

- Does Jack look at more apartments?

- Yes, he calls one more number.

- What is the name of the landlord?

- The man is named Mike.

- Does Jack know how to get to the house?

- Yes, he goes to the metro station. This apartment is located near the park.

- How long does Jack ride the subway?

- He rides the subway for about ten minutes.

- Does he immediately find the house?

- No, he cannot find the house, but he has an address.

- Can he ask somebody?

- Yes, he goes by a woman with a child.

- What does Jack ask her?

- He asks her how to get to the house.

- Does the woman know this house?

- Yes, she lives there. She points to Jack the

Richtung.

- Wo ist das Haus?

- Es ist hinter einer Bank.

- Gefällt Jack das Haus?

- Ja, es gefällt ihm, dass sich das Haus neben dem Park befindet.

- Befindet sich das Haus in einem ruhigen Ort?

- Ja, es ist still und ruhig rund um das Haus.

- In welcher Etage befindet sich Mikes Wohnung?

- Die Wohnung ist in der dritten Etage.

- Geht Jack treppauf?

- Nein, er fährt mit dem Aufzug. Er fährt zur dritten Etage.

- Klopft Jack an die Tür oder klingelt er?

- Er klingelt.

- Sind die Möbel in der Wohnung neu oder alt?

- Die Möbel in der Wohnung sind neu.

- Gibt es einen Fernseher im Zimmer?

- Ja, es gibt einen Großbildfernseher. Er ist neu.

- Wo ist das Bett in diesem Zimmer?

- Das Bett ist in der Zimmerecke.

- Welche Möbel gibt es im Zimmer?

- Es gibt ein großes Buchregal, in der Mitte gibt es einen Tisch und neben dem Tisch gibt es einen großen ledernen Sessel.

- Gefällt Jack die Wohnung?

- Ja, er sagt Mike, dass er hier wohnen will.

- Wieviel soll Jack für die Wohnung

direction in which to go.

- Where is the house?

- The house is located behind the bank.

- Does Jack like the house?

- Yes, he likes that the house is located next to the park.

- Is the house located in a quiet place?

- Yes, it is quiet and peaceful around the house.

- On what floor is Mike's apartment?

- Mike's apartment is on the third floor.

- Does Jack go up the stairs?

- No, Jack gets in the elevator. He goes to the third floor.

- Does Jack knock on the door or ring the bell?

- He rings the bell.

- Is furniture in the apartment new or old?

- The furniture in the apartment is new.

- Is there a TV in the room?

- Yes, there is a large TV. It is new.

- Where is the bed in the room?

- The bed is in the corner of the room.

- What furniture is in the room?

- There is a large bookcase in the living room, in the middle there is a table, and next to the table there is a big leather chair.

- Does Jack like the apartment?

- Yes, he says to Mike that he wants to live in this house.

- How much must Jack pay for the apartment?

bezahlen?

- Er soll Mike dreihundert Euro pro Monat bezahlen.

- Was beschließt Jack mit Mike?

- Sie schließen einen Vertrag.

- Für welche Periode muss Jack sofort bezahlen?

- Er muss für zwei Monaten sofort bezahlen.

- Wann zieht Jack vom Hotel um?

- Am gleichen Tag bringt er alle seinen Sachen aus dem Hotel.

- He must pay Mike three hundred euros per month.

- What does Jack conclude with Mike?

- They enter into a contract.

- For what period Jack must immediately pay?

- Jack has to pay for two months straight.

- When does he move from the hotel to the apartment?

- On the same day, he carries all his belongings out of the hotel.

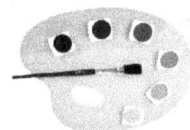

13

Im Geschäft

In the store

A

Vokabeln

1. Abteilung, die - aisle (in a store), section
2. Ananas, die - pineapple
3. aufstehen - to get up
4. auslegen - to display, to set out
5. Banane, die - banana
6. beschäftigt - busy
7. bezahlen - to pay
8. Boulevard, der - boulevard
9. Brötchen, das - breadroll, bun
10. Chips, die - (potato) chips
11. Ei, das - egg
12. Eingang, der - entry, entrance
13. entscheiden - to decide

14. Erdbeere, die - strawberry
15. essen - to eat
16. fahren - to drive, to transport, to take by
17. fertig - ready, prepared
18. Flasche, die - bottle
19. Fleisch- - meat (adj.)
20. funkionieren - to act, to work
21. gehen - to head
22. Geldtasche, die; das Portmonee - wallet
23. gelingen - to succeed, to go off well
24. Gemüse, das - vegetable
25. Gurke, die - cucumber
26. Hühner, die - chickens
27. Karotte, die - carrot(s)
28. Kasse, die - checkout, cash register
29. kassieren - to scan
30. Kohl, der - cabbage
31. leuchten, scheinen - to shine
32. Liter, der - liter
33. Milch- - dairy, milk (adj.)
34. nötig - necessary
35. Nudeln, die - pasta, macaroni
36. nur - only, just
37. Obst, das - fruit
38. Orange, die - orange
39. Orangen- - orange (adj.)
40. Päckchen, das - package
41. Paket, das - packet
42. Pfirsich, der - peach
43. Pilz, der - mushroom
44. Polyethylen- - polyethylene, plastic (adj.)
45. Rechnung, die - receipt
46. Regen, der - rain
47. Reis, der - rice
48. roh - raw
49. Saft, der - juice
50. Sahne, die - sour cream
51. Schachtel, die; die Kiste - box
52. Schlange, die - line, queue
53. Schublade, die - drawer, box
54. Sonne, die - sun
55. Sonntag, der - Sunday
56. Stand, der - rack, stand
57. Stück, das - piece
58. Tomate, die - tomato
59. Traube(n), die - grape(s)
60. verkauft werden - to be sold
61. verschieden - different, various
62. Waage, die - scales
63. Wagen, der - wagon, cart
64. wiegen - to weigh
65. Wurst, die - sausage
66. Zitrone, die - lemon

B

Heute ist Sonntag. Jack hat viel Freizeit. Er entscheidet sich, ins Geschäft zu gehen. Es ist zehn Uhr morgens. Jack steht auf. Er putzt seine Zähne, kleidet sich an und geht in die Küche, um zu frühstücken. Er will Lebensmittel für die Woche kaufen, also geht er in den Supermarkt. Der Supermarkt liegt in der Nähe. Jack geht draußen. Er geht dem Boulevard entlang. Draußen ist das Wetter gut. Die Sonne scheint. Viele Leute spazieren auf dem Boulevard. Jack geht weiter. Der Supermarkt ist schon nah. Er kommt ein. Jack nimmt einen Einkaufwagen. Er geht ins Geschäft und wählt Produkte. Jack ist in der Obstabteilung. Es gibt hier Bananen, Äpfel, Orangen, Ananasse, Pfirsiche, Erdbeeren und Trauben. Jack braucht Zitronen. Er nimmt eine Kunststofftüte und legt die Zitronen hinein. Jack nimmt drei. Er nimmt noch eine Kunststofftüte und legt dort die Äpfel hinein. Er nimmt fünf. Er legt die Tüten in den Wagen. Jack geht zu der Waage und wiegt das Obst. Er geht weiter. Er ist in der Gemüseabteilung. Es gibt hier Karotten, Tomaten, Pilze, Gurken, Kohl und noch mehr Gemüse. Sie liegen in Kisten. Jack will einige Tomaten und Gurken nehmen. Er nimmt das Gemüse und wiegt es. Dann geht Jack zur Fleischabteilung. Er will ein Stück Wurst nehmen. Jack wählt eine Wurst. Es gibt auch Fisch, rohe und fertige Hühnchen, Würste und andere Fleischprodukte. Jack geht weiter. Er nimmt ein Paket Eier. In der Nähe der Fleischabteilung nimmt er auch ein Paket Zucker. Er nimmt auch ein Paket Nudeln und ein Paket Reis. In der Milchabteilung nimmt Jack einen Karton Milch und einen Becher Sahne. In der

Today is Sunday. Jack has a lot of free time. He decides to go to the store. It's ten o'clock in the morning. Jack gets up from bed. He brushes his teeth, gets dressed and goes to have breakfast. He wants to buy food for a week, so he goes to the supermarket. There is a supermarket nearby. Jack leaves the house. He walks along the boulevard. Outside, the weather is good. The sun is shining. A lot of people are walking along the boulevard. Jack goes on. The supermarket is already close. He goes in. Jack takes a cart. He goes to the store and chooses food. Jack is in the produce aisle. There are bananas, apples, oranges, pineapples, peaches, strawberries and grapes. Jack needs lemons. He takes a plastic bag and puts lemons in. Jack takes three. He also takes another plastic bag and puts it in the apples. He takes five. He puts the bags in the cart. Jack brings the cart to the scales and weighs the fruit. Jack goes on. He is in the vegetable department. There are carrots, tomatoes, mushrooms, cucumbers, cabbage and other vegetables. They are in boxes. Jack wants to take some tomatoes and cucumbers. He is taking vegetables and weighing them. Then Jack goes to the meat department. He wants to take a piece of sausage. Jack chooses a sausage. There is also fish, raw and ready-chickens, sausages and other meat products. Jack goes on. He picks up a carton of eggs. Near the meat department, he takes a packet of sugar. He also takes a package of pasta and a package of rice. In the dairy department, Jack takes a carton of milk

Backwarenabteilung gibt es viele verschiedene Brötchen und Brote. Jack nimmt ein Brot und zwei süße Brötchen. Er nimmt auch ein kleines Paket Kekse. Jack geht zur Kasse. Auf dem Weg nimmt er noch zwei Flaschen Orangensaft mit. Es gibt einen Liter Saft in einer Flasche. Jack liebt auch Chips. Er kauft zwei Päckchen. Er geht mit dem Einkaufswagen zur Kasse. Es gibt eine lange Schlange zur Kasse. Jack steht in der Schlange. Jack stellt die Lebensmittel auf den Ladentisch. Der Kassierer scannt die Produkte. Jack will mit der Kreditkarte zahlen. Er gibt dem Kassierer seine Kreditkarte. Der Kassierer steckt die Karte in die Maschine, aber die Karte funktioniert nicht. Der Kassierer bittet Jack, mit Bargeld zu bezahlen. Jack hat etwas Geld in seinem Portmonee. Es reicht. Jack bezahlt dem Kassierer. Der Kassierer gibt ihm eine Rechnung. Jack verlässt das Geschäft.

and a cup of sour cream. In the bread department, there are a lot of different buns and bread. Jack picks up a loaf of bread and two sweet buns. He also takes one small box of cookies. Jack goes to the checkout. Along the way he picks up two bottles of orange juice. There is one liter of juice in a bottle. Jack also loves chips. He takes two packs. He carries the cart with the products to the checkout. There is a long line at the checkout. Jack stands in the queue. Jack puts food on the counter. The cashier scans the food. Jack wants to pay by credit card. He gives the cashier his card. Cashier puts the card through, but it does not work. The cashier asks Jack to pay in cash. Jack has a little money in his wallet. This is enough. Jack pays the cashier. The cashier gives him a check. Jack leaves the store.

 C

Fragen und Antworten

- Welcher Wochentag ist heute?
- Heute ist Sonntag.
- Ist Jack heute sehr beschäftigt?
- Nein, Jack hat viel Freizeit.
- Wohin geht Jack heute?
- Er entscheidet sich, ins Geschäft zu gehen.
- Wie spät ist es?
- Es ist zehn Uhr morgens.
- Warum geht Jack in den Supermarkt?
- Er will Lebensmittel für die Woche

Questions and Answers

- What day is it today?
- Today is Sunday.
- Is Jack very busy today?
- No, Jack has got a lot of free time.
- Where will Jack go today?
- He decides to go to the store.
- What time is it?
- It's ten o'clock in the morning.
- Why does Jack go to the supermarket?
- He wants to buy food for the week.

kaufen.

- Regnet es draußen?

- Nein, draußen ist das Wetter gut. Die Sonne scheint.

- Spazieren Leute auf dem Boulevard?

- Ja, viele Leute spazieren auf dem Boulevard.

- Was nimmt Jack am Supermarkteingang mit?

- Er nimmt einen Einkaufswagen mit.

- Was wird in der Obstabteilung verkauft?

- Es gibt Bananen, Äpfel, Orangen, Ananasse, Pfirsiche, Erdbeeren und Trauben.

- Was braucht Jack in dieser Abteilung?

- Er braucht Zitronen.

- Wie viele Zitronen legt er in die Kunststofftüte?

- Er nimmt drei.

- Was nimmt Jack noch?

- Er nimmt noch eine Kunststofftüte und legt Äpfel dort.

- Wie viele Äpfel nimmt Jack?

- Er nimmt fünf.

- Wo wiegt Jack das Obst?

- Er wiegt das Obst auf der Waage.

- Was gibt es in der Gemüseabteilung?

- Es gibt Karotten, Tomaten, Pilze, Gurken, Kohl und noch mehr Gemüse.

- Wo liegt das Gemüse?

- Es liegt in Kisten.

- Was für Gemüse braucht Jack?

- Is it raining outside?

- No, the weather is fine outside. The sun is shining.

- Are there people walking along the boulevard?

- Yes, a lot of people are walking along the boulevard.

- What does Jack take at the entrance to the supermarket?

- Jack takes a cart.

- What is sold in the fruit department?

- There are bananas, apples, oranges, pineapple, peaches, strawberries and grapes.

- What does Jack need in this department?

- Jack needs lemons.

- How many lemons does he put in a plastic bag?

- He puts three.

- What else does Jack take?

- He takes another plastic bag and puts apples in it.

- How many apples does Jack take?

- He takes five.

- Where does Jack weigh the fruit?

- Jack fruit weighs on the scale.

- What is there in the vegetable department?

- There are carrots, tomatoes, mushrooms, cucumbers, cabbage and other vegetables.

- Where are the vegetables?

- They are in boxes.

- What vegetables does Jack need?

- Jack will einige Tomaten und Gurken nehmen.
- Nimmt Jack das Gemüse und geht weiter?
- Nein, er nimmt das Gemüse und wiegt es.
- Will Jack ein Stück Wurst in der Fleischabteilung nehmen?
- Ja, Jack wählt die Wurst.
- Welche Produkte nimmt Jack noch?
- Er nimmt einen Karton Eier, ein Paket Zucker, ein Paket Nudeln und ein Paket Reis.
- Isst Jack Milchprodukte?
- Ja, Jack nimmt einen Karton Milch und einen Becher Sahne in der Milchabteilung.
- Gibt es eine gute Backwarenabteilung im Supermarkt?
- Ja, in der Backwarenabteilung gibt es viele verschiedene Brötchen und Brote.
- Kauft Jack nur Brot oder kauft er noch Brötchen?
- Jack nimmt ein Brot und zwei süße Brötchen.
- Mag er Kekse?
- Ja, er nimmt ein kleines Paket Kekse.
- Was nimmt Jack noch auf dem Weg zur Kasse mit?
- Auf dem Weg zur Kasse nimmt er zwei Flaschen Saft mit.
- Welchen Saft kauft Jack?
- Orangensaft.
- Wieviel Saft gibt es in einer Flasche?
- In einer Flasche gibt es einen Liter Saft.
- Mag Jack Chips?

- Jack wants to take a few tomatoes and cucumbers.
- Does Jack take the vegetables and go further?
- No, he picks up vegetables and weighs them.
- Does Jack want to take a piece of sausage in the meat section?
- Yes, Jack chooses sausage.
- What other products does Jack take?
- He takes a carton of eggs, a packet of sugar, a packet of pasta and a pack of rice.
- Does Jack eat dairy products?
- Yes, Jack takes a carton of milk and a cup of sour cream in the dairy department.
- Is there a good bread department in the supermarket?
- Yes, there are a lot of different buns and bread in the bread department.
- Does Jack only buy bread or does he buy buns too?
- Jack picks up a loaf of bread and two sweet buns.
- Does he like cookies?
- Yes, he takes one small box of cookies.
- What else does Jack take on the way to the checkout?
- On the way to the checkout, he takes two bottles of juice.
- What kind of juice does Jack buy?
- Orange juice.
- How much juice is there in a bottle?
- There is one liter of juice in a bottle.

- Ja, er liebt Chips. Er nimmt zwei Päckchen.

- Gibt es eine Schlange an der Kasse?

- Ja, es gibt eine lange Schlange an der Kasse.

- Will Jack nicht Schlange stehen und geht er ohne Lebensmittel weg?

- Nein, er steht Schlange.

- Wohin legt er die Produkte?

- Er legt die Produkte auf den Ladentisch.

- Will Jack mit Bargeld oder mit der Kreditkarte zahlen?

- Er will mit der Kreditkarte bezahlen. Er gibt dem Kassierer seine Karte.

- Gelingt es ihm, mit der Kreditkarte für die Produkte zu zahlen?

- Nein. Der Kassierer steckt die Karte in die Maschine, aber sie funktioniert nicht.

- Worum bittet der Kassierer Jack?

- Der Kassierer bittet Jack, mit Bargeld zu zahlen.

- Hat Jack Geld?

- Er hat etwas Geld in seinem Portmonee.

- Ist es genug, um für die Produkte zu bezahlen?

- Ja, es reicht. Jack bezahlt dem Kassierer.

- Does Jack like chips?

- Yes, Jack loves chips. He takes two packs.

- Is there a line at the checkout?

- Yes, there is a long line at the checkout.

- Does Jack not want to stand in the line and leaves without the food?

- No, Jack stands in the line.

- Where did he puts food?

- Jack puts food on the counter.

- Does Jack want to pay in cash or by credit card?

- Jack wants to pay by credit card. He gives the cashier his card.

- Does he manage to pay for products by card?

- No. The cashier puts the card through, but it does not work.

- What does the cashier ask Jack?

- The cashier asks Jack to pay in cash.

- Does Jack have money?

- He has a little money in his wallet.

- Does he have enough money to him to pay?

- Yes, he has enough money. Jack pays the cashier.

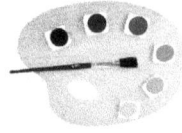

14

Heute habe ich vier Fächer

I have four classes today

 A

Vokabeln

1. Abend, der - evening
2. anderthalb - one and a half
3. Anfang, der - beginning
4. anfangen, beginnen - to start
5. anziehen - to put on
6. aufmerksam - carefully, attentively
7. ausschreiben - to write out (a check)
8. belegte Brot, das - sandwich
9. Bibliothekar, der - librarian
10. Biologie, die - biology
11. bleiben - to be left, to stay
12. Bleistift, der - pencil
13. Brett, das - board
14. Brüssel - Brussels
15. Büro, das - office
16. dauern - to take (time), to last

17. Dekanat, das - dean's office
18. Fach, das; das Ding - subject, thing
19. Formel, die - formula
20. Frieden, der; die Welt - peace; world
21. Frühstück, das - breakfast
22. Geographie, die; die Erdkunde - geography
23. Geschichte, die - history
24. greifen - to reach
25. heiß - hot
26. Hörsaal, der - auditorium, class-room
27. in - in, into
28. interessant - interesting
29. Kreide, die - chalk
30. Lehrbuch, das - textbook
31. Lehrer, der - teacher, instructor
32. leicht - light
33. Lineal, das - ruler
34. müde werden - to get tired
35. nächster - following, next
36. notieren - to write down
37. öffnen - to open
38. Oma, die; die alte Frau - grandmother, old woman
39. Opa, der; der alte Mann - grandfather, old man
40. Ozean, der - ocean
41. Paar, das - pair
42. Pause, die - break
43. Physik, die - physics
44. Prüfung, die - test
45. Rechnung, die - bill
46. Regel, die - rule
47. Seite, die - page
48. sich vorbereiten - to prepare oneself
49. (Treppen)Stufe, die - step
50. über - about
51. Unterricht, das; die Kurse, die Fächer - classes
52. vierter - fourth
53. Zeitschrift, die - magazine
54. zurückgeben - to return
55. Zusammenfassung, die; das Resümee - synopsis, outline
56. zwölfter - twelfth

B

Heute gehe ich zur Universität. Ich muss dort um halb neun sein. Ich ziehe mich an. Draußen ist es heiß, deshalb nehme ich dünne Kleidung. Dann esse ich das Frühstück. Zum Frühstück esse ich ein belegtes Brot und trinke ich Tee. Ich sammle meine Sachen ein. Ich nehme mein Heft, einen Kugelschreiber,

Today I'm going to university. I have to be there at eight thirty. I get dressed. It is hot outside, so I put on light clothing. Then I have breakfast. I eat a sandwich and drink tea for breakfast. I collect my things. I take with me a notebook, pen, pencil, ruler and history textbook to

einen Bleistift, ein Lineal und ein Geschichtslehrbuch mit zur Universität. Ich verlasse die Wohnung und gehe zur Bushaltestelle. Ich steige in den Bus ein und fahre zur Universität. Ich sehe die Universität. Neben dem Eingang gibt es viele Studenten. Ich gehe zur Tür und trete ein. Heute habe ich vier Fächer. Das erste - Physik, das zweite - Geschichte, das dritte - Biologie, das vierte - Englisch. Ich muss zum Hörsaal für die Physikunterricht gehen. Ich gehe treppauf bis zur zweiten Etage. Viele Studenten stehen vor dem Hörsaal. Das Unterricht fängt in zehn Minuten an. Ich gehe in den Hörsaal und setze mich. Neben mir sitzt mein Freund Mike. Er hat sehr gute Noten. Der Lehrer kommt herein. Er heißt Herr Steven. Er nimmt die Kreide und schreibt das Thema auf die Tafel. Studenten nehmen ihre Hefte und Kugelschreiber heraus. Wir notieren das Thema. Herr Steven gibt uns dann unsere Physiklehrbücher. Er bittet uns, die Bücher auf der zwölften Seite zu öffnen. Wir notieren die Formeln und Regeln in unseren Heften. Herr Steven erklärt uns das Thema. Wir hören aufmerksam. Das Unterricht dauert anderthalb Stunden. Dann verlasse ich den Hörsaal. Die Pause beginnt. Die Pause dauert fünfzehn Minuten. Dann ist die Geschichte. Ich muss auf die dritte Etage gehen. Dort ist der Raum für Geschichte. Ich gehe treppauf und dann in den Saal. Unser Lehrer heißt Herr Oliven. Er sitzt am Tisch und liest eine Zeitung. Eine große Landkarte hängt an der Tafel in seinem Raum. Studenten kommen in den Saal und setzen sich auf ihre Plätze. Die Vorlesung fängt an. Der Lehrer schaut auf die Karte. Er erzählt uns die Geschichte der Stadt Brüssel. Dann schreibt er das Thema an die Tafel. Die Vorlesung dauert anderthalb Stunden. Wir gehen aus dem Saal. Die lange Pause fängt an. Sie dauert eine halbe Stunde.

university. I leave the house and go to the bus stop. I get on the bus to university. I see the university. There are a lot of students at the entrance. I go to the door and enter the university. Today I have four classes. The first lesson is physics, the second one is history, the third one is biology, the fourth one is English. I need to go to the auditorium for physics. I climb the stairs to the second floor. I go to the physics auditory. A lot of students are standing near the auditorium. Ten minutes remain before the beginning of the class. I go into the auditorium and sit down on a chair. Sitting next to me is my friend Mike. He gets very good grades. Our teacher comes in. His name is Mr. Steven. He picks up the chalk and writes a topic on the board. Students take out their notebooks and pens. We write down the topic. Mr. Steven then distributes our books on physics. He asks us to open the books on page twelve. We write down formulas and rules in our notebooks. Mr. Steven tells us about the topic. We listen carefully. The class lasts an hour and a half. Then I leave the auditorium. The break has started. The break lasts fifteen minutes. Next is the history lesson. I need to go to the third floor. The history classroom is there. I go up to the third floor and I go into the classroom. Our teacher is called Mr. Oliven. He is sitting at a table and is reading a newspaper. A large map hangs on the blackboard in his room. Students come to the room and sit down in their seats. The class begins. Our teacher looks at a map. He tells us the history of the city of Brussels. He then writes a topic on the board. The class lasts an

Ich gehe aus der Universität und in ein Café. Mein Freund Mike kommt mit. Das Café liegt in der Nähe. Wir kommen in das Café. Ich bestelle Pizza und Kaffee. Ich sitze mit Mike zwanzig Minute lang im Café. Dann bezahle ich den Kellner und gehe nach draußen. In der dritten Stunde haben wir Biologie. Ich liebe es, zu Biologievorlesungen zu gehen. Unser Lehrer Herr Christin erzählt sehr interessante Dinge. Die Vorlesung dauert anderthalb Stunden. Dann gehe ich zum Englischunterricht. Ich spreche Englisch gut. Meine Großeltern wohnen in England. Ich fahre oft dorthin, um sie zu besuchen. Ich denke daran, nach dem Unterricht in die Bibliothek zu gehen. Morgen habe ich einen Test in Geographie, ich muss mich also gut vorbereiten. Ich will ein Buch über die Ozeane der Welt ausleihen. Ich muss eine Zusammenfassung schreiben. Die Bibliothek befindet sich in unserer Universität. Sie ist in der vierten Etage. Ich gehe in die Bibliothek. Viele Studenten sitzen dort. Sie lesen und machen Notizen. Es ist schon vier Uhr nachmittags. Ich bin müde. Ich will die Bücher nach Hause mitnehmen. Ich gehe zum Bibliothekar. Ich bitte ihn, mir ein Buch über die Ozeane zu zeigen. Der Bibliothekar zeigt mir drei Bücher. Ich schaue sie an. Ich entscheide mich, zwei Bücher mitzunehmen. Ich nehme auch eine Zeitschrift. Ich leihe die Bücher und die Zeitschrift aus. Der Bibliothekar sagt, dass ich die Bücher und die Zeitschrift in drei Wochen zurückgeben soll. Ich nehme die Bücher und die Zeitschrift und gehe nach Hause.

hour and a half. Then we go out of the room. The long break begins. It lasts thirty minutes. I go out of the university and go to a cafe. My friend Mike goes with me. The cafe is located nearby. We come into the cafe. I order a pizza and coffee. I sit in the cafe with Mike for twenty minutes. Then I pay the bill for the food to the waiter and leave the cafe. The third lesson is in biology. I love to go to lectures on biology. Our instructor Mr. Christin tells very interesting things. The lecture lasts an hour and a half. Then I go to the English class. I know English well. My grandparents live in England. I often go to visit them. I think I'll go to the library after classes. Tomorrow I have a test in geography, so I need to prepare well. I want to take a book on the world's oceans. I need to make an outline. The library is located at our university. It is on the fourth floor. I go to the library. A lot of students are sitting in the library. They are reading and taking notes. It's already four o'clock in the afternoon. I'm tired. So I want to take the books home. I go to the librarian. I ask him to show me a book about the oceans. The librarian shows me three books. I look at the books. I decide to take two of them home. I also take a magazine. I check out the books and the magazine. The librarian says that I have to return the books and the magazine in three weeks. I take the books and the magazine, and go home.

C

Fragen und Antworten	**Questions and Answers**
- Wohin gehst du heute?	- Where are you going today?
- Ich gehe zur Universität.	- Today I'm going to university.
- Wie spät musst du dort sein?	- At what time do you have to be there?
- Ich muss um halb neun dort sein.	- I have to be there at half past eight.
- Warum nimmst du dünne Kleidung?	- Why do you wear light clothing?
- Ich nehme dünne Kleidung, weil es draußen heiß ist.	- I wear light clothing because it is hot outside.
- Was isst du zum Frühstück?	- What do you eat for breakfast?
- Ich esse ein belegtes Brot und trinke Tee zum Frühstück.	- For breakfast I eat a sandwich and drink tea.
- Was nimmst du mit zur Universität?	- What do you take with you to university?
- Ich nehme ein Heft, einen Kugelschreiber, einen Bleistift, ein Lineal und das Geschichtslehrbuch mit.	- I take a notebook, pen, pencil, ruler and history textbook to university.
- Gehst du zur Universität zu Fuß oder fährst du mit dem Bus?	- Do you get on foot or by bus to university?
- Ich fahre mit dem Bus zur Universität.	- I get to university by bus.
- Wie viele Stunden Unterricht hast du heute?	- How many classes do you have today?
- Heute habe ich vier Stunden.	- Today I have four classes.
- Welche Fächer studierst du?	- What subjects do you study?
- Physik, Geschichte, Biologie und Englisch.	- Physics, history, biology and English.
- Zu welcher Etage musst du gehen?	- To which floor do you have to get?
- Ich gehe treppauf zur zweiten Etage.	- I climb the stairs to the second floor.
- Gehst du zum Dekan?	- Do you go to the dean?
- Nein, ich gehe in den Physikhörsaal.	- No, I'm going to the physics auditorium.
- Wie viele Minuten bleiben noch zum Anfang des Unterrichts?	- How many minutes are left before the start of classes?

- Zehn Minuten bleiben noch zum Unterricht.
- Wer sitzt neben dir?
- Mein Freund Mike sitzt neben mir.
- Hat er gute Noten?
- Ja, er hat sehr gute Noten.
- Wie heißt dein Lehrer?
- Sein Name ist Herr Steven.
- Wie beginnt Herr Steven die Unterricht?
- Er schreibt das Thema an die Tafel.
- Was gibt Herr Steven aus?
- Er gibt Physiklehrbücher aus.
- Auf welcher Seite öffnet ihr das Buch?
- Wir öffnen das Buch auf der zwölften Seite.
- Was notiert ihr in euren Heften?
- Wir notieren Formeln und Regeln in unseren Heften.
- Hört ihr Herrn Steven aufmerksam zu?
- Ja, wir hören ihm aufmerksam zu.
- Wie lange dauert das Unterricht?
- Das Unterricht dauert anderthalb Stunden.
- Wie lang ist die Pause?
- Die Pause dauert fünfzehn Minuten.
- Auf welcher Etage ist der Raum für Geschichtsunterricht?
- Der Raum ist in der dritten Etage.
- Wie heißt euer Lehrer?
- Sein Name ist Herr Oliven.
- Was macht er während der Pause?

- There are ten minutes before the class.
- Who is sitting next to you?
- My friend Mike is sitting next to me.
- Does he do well at university?
- Yes, he does very well.
- What is the name of your teacher?
- His name is Mr. Steven.
- How does Mr. Steven start class?
- Mr. Steven writes the topic on the board.
- What does Mr. Steven distribute?
- Mr. Steven distributes our books on physics.
- On which page do you open the book?
- We open the book on page twelve.
- What do you write in your notebook?
- We write formulas and rules in our notebooks.
- Do you listen to Mr. Steven carefully?
- Yes, we listen to him carefully.
- How long does a lesson last?
- A lesson lasts an hour and a half.
- How long is the break?
- Break lasts fifteen minutes.
- On what floor is the history room?
- The room is on the third floor.
- What is your teacher's name?
- Our teacher's name is Mr. Oliven.
- What does he do during the break?

- Er sitzt am Tisch und liest eine Zeitung.
- Was hängt an der Tafel im Raum für den Geschichtsunterricht?
- Eine große Landkarte hängt an der Tafel.
- Worüber spricht der Lehrer?
- Er erzählt die Geschichte der Stadt Brüssel.
- Wie lange dauert die große Pause?
- Sie dauert dreißig Minuten.
- Wer geht mit dir ins Café?
- Mein Freund Mike geht mit.
- Ist das Café weit?
- Nein, es ist nah.
- Was bestellst du?
- Ich bestelle Pizza und Kaffee.
- Wie lange sitzt ihr im Café?
- Ich sitze mit Mike zwanzig Minuten lang im Café.
- Wen bezahlst du für das Essen?
- Ich bezahle den Kellner.
- Magst du Biologieunterricht?
- Ja, ich mag es, zum Biologieunterricht zu gehen.
- Heißt dein Lehrer Herr Christin?
- Ja, er heißt Herr Christin.
- Erzählt er alles auf eine interessante Art?
- Ja, unser Lehrer Herr Christin macht alles sehr interessant.
- Sprichst du Englisch?
- Ja, ich spreche Englisch.
- Wo sind deine Großeltern?

- He sits at the table and reads a newspaper.
- What hangs on the blackboard in the history room?
- A large map hangs on the blackboard.
- What does the teacher tell you about?
- He tells us the history of the city of Brussels.
- How long is the big break?
- It lasts thirty minutes.
- Who goes with you to the cafe?
- My friend Mike goes with me.
- Is the cafe far?
- No, the cafe is next door.
- What do you order?
- I order a pizza and coffee.
- How long do you sit in the cafe?
- I sit in the cafe with Mike for twenty minutes.
- To whom do you pay the bill for the food?
- I pay the bill for the food to the waiter.
- Do you like biology classes?
- Yes, I like to go to biology classes.
- Is your teacher's name Mr. Christin?
- Yes, his name is Mr. Christin.
- Does he tells things in an interesting way?
- Yes, our teacher Mr. Christin makes things very interesting.
- Do you speak English?
- Yes, I speak English.
- Where are your grandparents?

- Meine Großeltern wohnen in England.	- My grandparents live in England.
- Besuchst du sie?	- Do you go to visit them?
- Ja, ich besuche sie oft.	- Yes, I often go to visit them.
- Wohin willst du nach dem Unterricht gehen?	- Where do you want to go after classes?
- Ich denke daran, in die Bibliothek zu gehen.	- I think I'll go to the library.
- In welchem Fach hast du morgen einen Test?	- In what subject do you have a test tomorrow?
- Morgen habe ich einen Test in Geographie.	- Tomorrow I have a test in geography.
- Musst du dich vorbereiten?	- Do you need to prepare for it?
- Ja, ich muss mich gut vorbereiten.	- Yes, I need to prepare well.
- Welche Bücher musst du aus der Bibliothek verleihen?	- What kind of books do you want to take out of the library?
- Ich brauche ein Buch über die Ozeane der Welt.	- I want to take a book on the world's oceans.
-Wofür brauchst du diese Bücher?	- Why do you need these books?
- Ich muss eine Zusammenfassung schreiben.	- I need to write an outline.
- Wo ist die Bibliothek?	- Where is the library?
- Die Bibliothek befindet sich in unserer Universität auf der vierten Etage.	- The library is in our university on the fourth floor.
- Wie viele Studenten gibt es in der Bibliothek?	- How many students are in the library?
- Es gibt viele Studenten in der Bibliothek.	- A lot of students sit in the library.
- Was machen sie?	- What do they do?
- Sie lesen und machen Notizen.	- They read and take notes.
- Nimmst du ein Buch und setzst du dich, um eine Zusammenfassung zu schreiben?	- Do you take a book and sit down to write an outline in the library?
- Nein, ich bin müde, also will ich die Bücher nach Hause mitnehmen.	- No, I'm tired, so I want to take the books home.
- Worum bittest du den Bibliothekar?	- What do you ask the librarian?

- Ich bitte ihn, mir ein Buch über die Ozeane zu zeigen.

- Wie viele Bücher willst du nach Hause mitnehmen?

- Ich entscheide mich, zwei Bücher mitzunehmen.

- Nimmst du auch eine Zeitschrift?

- Ja, ich nehme auch eine Zeitschrift.

- Wann musst du die Bücher und die Zeitschrift zurückgeben?

- Der Bibliothekar sagt, ich muss die Bücher und die Zeitschrift in drei Wochen zurückgeben.

- I ask him to show me a book about oceans.

- How many books do you decide to take home?

- I decide to take two books home.

- Do you also take a magazine?

- Yes, I also take a magazine.

- When do you have to return the books and magazine?

- The librarian says that I have to return the books and magazine in three weeks.

15

Jack will eine Teilzeitarbeit finden

Jack wants to work part-time

A

Vokabeln

1. aktiv - active
2. Alter, das - age
3. anbieten - to suggest, to offer
4. Anstellung, die - placement, employment
5. Arbeits- - work (adj.)
6. Ausbildung, die; die Erziehung - education
7. ausfüllen - to fill out
8. ausgefüllt - filled out
9. danke - thanks
10. einen Job finden - to get a job
11. Erfahrung, die - experience
12. Familien- - family (adj.)
13. Familienname, der - last name
14. Fertigkeit, die; die Kenntnis - skill
15. fließend - free(ly), fluently

16. Fragebogen, der - questionnaire
17. früher - before, earlier
18. Führerschein - driving license
19. gesellig - sociable
20. Hallo - hello
21. Handarbeit, die - physical work
22. (in) Teilzeit - part-time
23. klopfen - to knock
24. Leiter, der; der Chef - manager, head
25. machen - do, carry out
26. Mädchen, das - girl
27. männlich - male
28. Name, der - name
29. Niederländer, der - Dutchman
30. niederländisch - Dutch (adj.)
31. Person, die; der Mensch - person
32. persönlich - personal
33. Rechte, die - rights
34. sich einrichten - to settle
35. Sitz- - sitting
36. Stand, der; der Status - status
37. Teilzeitarbeit, die - part-time job
38. Telefon, das - phone
39. tragen - to carry
40. Transportarbeiter, der; der Packer - loader, stevedore
41. verdienen - to earn
42. verheiratet - married (for men)
43. versprechen - to promise
44. voll - full
45. Werbung, die - commercial, advertisement
46. werden - to become
47. wünschen - to wish, to desire

B

Jack hat wenig Geld. Er will eine Teilzeitarbeit finden. Er hat Freizeit nach dem Unterricht. Sein Freund Mike arbeitet als Lader in einem Supermarkt nach der Universität. Mike verdient dreißig Euro pro Tag. Jack fragt Mike, wie er diese Arbeit gefunden hat. Mike sagt Jack, dass es bei der Arbeitsagentur gewesen ist. Dort wurde ihm die Arbeit angeboten. Mike gibt Jack die Adresse der Agentur. Jack entscheidet sich, zur Arbeitsagentur zu gehen. Die Agentur befindet sich im Zentrum. Jack fährt dorthin mit der U-Bahn. Er findet das Büro schnell.

Jack has little money. He wants to work part-time. He has free time after university classes. His friend Mike works as a loader in a supermarket after school. Mike gets thirty euros per day. Jack asks Mike how he found the job. Mike tells Jack that he went to an employment agency. There he was offered the job. Mike gives Jack the address of the agency. Jack also decides to go to the employment agency. The agency is located in the city center. Jack gets there by subway. He quickly finds the agency. A lot of ads about work

Am Eingang hängen viele Anzeigen für Studentenarbeit. Jack kommt hinein. Dort sieht er eine lange Schlange. Es sind Leute, die auch eine Arbeit finden wollen. Sie stehen neben dem Schalter. Die Menschen nehmen Personalfragebogen mit. Jack stellt sich an das Ende der Schlange. In fünfzehn Minuten ist er an der Reihe.

„Hallo. Ich bin Lisa", sagt das Mädchen im Schalter zu Jack.

„Hallo. Ich bin Jack", sagt Jack.

„Suchst du eine Arbeit?", fragt ihn das Mädchen.

„Ja", antwortet Jack.

„Willst du eine Vollzeitarbeit oder eine Teilzeitarbeit?", fragt das Mädchen.

„Ich studiere und will nach dem Unterricht arbeiten", sagt Jack.

„Nimm, bitte, den Fragebogen für Studenten und fülle ihn aus. Wenn der Fragebogen ausgefüllt ist, gib ihn der Abteilungschefin", sagt das Mädchen und gibt ihm einen Fragebogen.

„Danke", sagt Jack und nimmt den Fragebogen.

Jack nimmt einen Kugelschreiber und füllt den Fragebogen aus.

Name - Jack

Familienname - Stroman

Geschlecht - männlich

Alter - neunzehn Jahre alt

Staatsangehörigkeit - niederländisch

Familienstand - ledig

Ausbildung - Ich studiere an der Universität für Technologie und Design.

for students hangs at the entrance. Jack goes inside. There he sees a long queue. These are people who also want to get a job. They stand at the help desk. People take questionnaires for personal data. Jack stands in the line. Jack's turn comes in fifteen minutes.

"Hello, my name is Lisa," says the girl at the help desk to Jack.

"Hello, I am Jack," Jack says.

"Are you looking for work?" the girl asks him.

"Yes," Jack says.

"Do you want to work full-time or part-time?" the girl asks.

"I am a student and I want to work after classes," Jack says.

"Then take and complete the questionnaire for students, please. When you complete the questionnaire, take it to the head of department," the girl says and gives him a questionnaire.

"Thank you," Jack says and takes the form.

Jack picks up a pen and fills out the questionnaire.

Name - Jack

Surname - Stroman

Gender - Male

Age - Nineteen years old

Nationality - Dutch

Marital status - Single

Education - I study at the University of Technology and Design.

Previous work - I have not worked

Frühere Arbeit - Ich habe nicht gearbeitet.

Welche Kenntnisse und Erfahrungen haben Sie? - Ich bin eine aktive und gesellige Person. Ich kann manuelle Arbeiten machen. Ich kann auch mit dem Computer arbeiten.

Sprachen (0 - nicht, 10 - fließend) - Englisch - 7, Deutsch - 10, Niederländisch - 10

Führerschein - nein

Lohnerwartung - 30-40 Euro pro Tag

Telefonnummer - +3456787487

Jack nimmt den Fragebogen und geht zum Büro der Abteilungschefin. Er klopft und tritt ein.

„Guten Tag, ich heiße Jack. Man hat mir gesagt, meinen Fragebogen der Abteilungschefin abzugeben", sagt Jack zu der Frau, die am Schreibtisch sitzt.

„Guten Tag, ich heiße Eva Steg. Ich bin die Abteilungschefin. Bitte geben sie mir den Fragebogen", sie antwortet.

„Bitte", sagt Jack und gibt ihr seinen Fragebogen. "Wann kann ich eine Arbeit erwarten?"

„Wir werden Sie anrufen, wenn wir für Sie eine Arbeit finden", sie sagt.

before.

What skills and experience do you have? - I am an active and sociable person. I can do physical work. I can also do work on the computer.

Languages (0 - no, 10 - fluent) - English 7, German 10, Dutch 10

Driving license - No

Salary expectations - 30-40 euro per day

Phone number - +3456787487

Jack takes the form and goes to the office of the head of department. He knocks and comes into the office.

"Hello, my name is Jack. I was told to give the head of the department my questionnaire," says Jack to the woman sitting at the desk.

"Hello, my name is Eva Steg. I am the head of this department. You can give me your questionnaire," she answers.

"Here you are," Jack says, handing over his questionnaire. "When can I get a job?"

"We'll call you when we find a job for you," she says.

Fragen und Antworten

- Hat Jack viel Geld?
- Nein, Jack hat wenig Geld.
- Will Jack eine Arbeit finden?
- Ja, er will Geld verdienen.

Questions and Answers

- Does Jack have a lot of money?
- No, Jack has little money.
- Does Jack want to get a job?
- Yes, he wants to earn money.

- Hat er Zeit für eine Teilzeitarbeit?

- Ja, er hat Zeit nach dem Unterricht.

- Was macht sein Freund Mike?

- Er arbeitet als Packer in einem Supermarkt nach dem Unterricht.

- Wie viel Geld verdient Mike?

- Er verdient dreißig Euro pro Tag.

- Fragt Jack seinen Freund, wo er die Arbeit gefunden hat?

- Ja, Mike gibt Jack die Adresse der Arbeitsagentur.

- Wo ist die Agentur?

- Die Agentur befindet sich im Zentrum.

- Fährt Jack dorthin mit dem Bus?

- Nein, Jack fährt mit der U-Bahn dorthin.

- Was sieht Jack am Eingang zur Agentur?

- Viele Anzeigen für Studentenarbeit hängen am Eingang.

- Gibt es viele Leute in der Agentur?

- Ja, er sieht eine lange Schlange.

- Wer sind diese Leute?

- Es sind Leute, die auch eine Arbeit suchen.

- Was nehmen die Leute?

- Die Leute nehmen Personalfragebogen.

- Wie lange wartet Jack?

- Jack steht Schlange für fünfzehn Minuten.

- Will Jack Vollzeit arbeiten oder such er eine Teilzeitarbeit?

- Jack studiert und will nach dem Unterricht arbeiten.

- Does he have time for part-time work?

- Yes, he has free time after university classes.

- What does his friend Mike do?

- His friend Mike works as a loader in a supermarket after university classes.

- How much money does Mike get?

- Mike gets thirty euros per day.

- Does Jack ask Mike where he found the job?

- Yes, Mike gives Jack address of an employment agency.

- Where is this agency?

- The agency is located in the city center.

- Does Jack go there by bus?

- No, Jack gets there by subway.

- What does Jack see at the entrance to the agency?

- Many ads about work for students are hanging at the entrance.

- Are there many people at the agency?

- Yes, there he sees a long line.

- Who are these people?

- These are people who also want to get a job.

- What do people take?

- People take personal questionnaires.

- How much time does Jack stand in the line?

- Jack stands in the line for fifteen minutes.

- Does Jack want to work full-time or part-time?

- Jack is a university student and wants to

- Wem gibt Jack den ausgefüllten Fragebogen?

- Er gibt den Fragebogen der Abteilungschefin.

- Wie schnell kann Jack eine Arbeit erwarten?

- Die Abteilungschefin verspricht, ihn anzurufen, wenn sie eine Arbeit für ihn finden.

work after classes.

- To whom does Jack give the completed application form?

- Jack gives the form to the head of the department.

- How soon can Jack get a job?

- They promise to call Jack when they find a job for him.

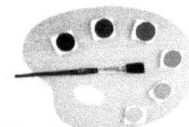

Wörterbuch Deutsch-Englisch

Abend, der - evening
abends, am Abend - in the evening
Abenteuer, das - adventure
aber, doch, und - but, while, and
ablehnen - to refuse
absagen - to refuse
abschneiden - to cut off
Abteilung, die - aisle (in a store), section
acht - eight
achthundert - eight hundred
achtzehn - eighteen
Addresse, die - address
Agentur, die; das Büro - agency
aktiv - active
Alkohol- - alcoholic
alles - all, everything
alt - old
älter - older
Alter, das - age
Ampel, die - traffic lights
Ananas, die - pineapple
anbieten - to suggest, to offer
andere(r/s) - other
anderthalb - one and a half
Anfang, der - beginning
anfangen, beginnen - to start
Angaben, die - data, information
angezeigt - indicated
anrufen - to call (by phone)
anschauen - to watch

Anstellung, die; die Beschäftigung - employment, job, placement
antworten - to answer
Anzeige, die - announcement, ad
anzeigen, andeuten - to indicate
anziehen - to put on
Apfel, der - apple
Apotheke, die - drugstore
Arbeit, die - work
arbeiten, funktionieren - to work, function
Arbeiter, der - worker
Arbeits- - work (adj.)
Arzt, der - doctor, physician
auch - also, too
auf - on
auf Deutsch - in German
auf Englisch - in English
auf Französisch - in French
auf Spanisch - in Spanish
aufmerksam - carefully, attentively
aufräumen - to clean, to tidy up
aufschreiben - to write (down)
aufstehen - to get up, to wake up
aufwärmen - to warm (up)
Aufzug, der - elevator
aus, von - from, out of
Ausbildung, die; die Erziehung - education
ausfahren - to drive out
ausfüllen - to fill out
Ausgang, der - exit

ausgefüllt - filled out

Ausguss, der; das Becken - sink

Auskunfts- - information (adj.), referential (adj.)

auslegen - to display, to set out

ausschreiben - to write out (a check)

aussehen - to look (like)

Auto, das; der Wagen - automobile, car; Auto- - automobile (adj.)

Autobahn, die - highway

Autoservice, der - car service

Badewanne, die - bathtub

Badezimmer, das; das Bad - bathroom

bald - soon

Banane, die - banana

Bank, die - bank; Bank- - bank (adjective)

Bar, die; die Gaststätte - bar

Bargeld, das - cash

Basketball, der - basketball

Baum, der - tree

(be)zahlen - to pay

begleiten; verbringen - to accompany; to spend (time)

behandelt werden - to get treated

Behandlung, die - treatment

bei, an - at, near

beigefarben, beige (unflektiert), sandfarbig - beige

bekommen, nach etwas greifen - to get, to reach, to take something out

belegte Brot, das; die Schnitte - sandwich

bequem - comfortable

Berater, der - consultant

Berg, der - hill, mountain

Beruf, der; das Fach - profession

beschäftigt - busy

besprechen - to discuss

besser - better

bestellen - to order

Bett, das - bed

bezahlen - to pay

Bibliothek, die; die Bücherei - library

Bibliothekar, der - librarian

Bild, das - picture

Biologie, die - biology

bis - until, to

blau - blue

bleiben - to be left, to stay

Bleistift, der - pencil

Blender, der - blender

Blume, die - flower

Boulevard, der - boulevard

brauchen - to be necessary, to need to

braun - brown

brennen - to burn

Brett, das - board

Briefmarke, die - stamp

Brille, die - glasses

Brot, das - bread

Brötchen, das - breadroll, bun

Brücke, die - bridge

Bruder, der - brother

Brüssel - Brussels

Buch- - book (adj.); Buch, das - book

Bürgersteig, der; der Fußweg - sidewalk

Büro, das - office
Bürste, die - brush
Bus- - bus (adj.); Bus, der - bus
Café, das - cafe
Cerealien, die - flakes, cereal
Chips, die - (potato) chips
Computer, der - computer
Dach, das - roof
damals, dann - then
danke - thanks
dann - afterwards, then, later
das - this
dauern - to take (time), to last
Decke, die - ceiling
dein - your(s)
Dekanat, das - dean's office
denken - to think
Denkmal, das - memorial, monument
deshalb - so, because of this
Dessert, das; der Nachtisch - cake, dessert
Detektiv, der - detective
Deutsch - German
diese - this (feminine), these (plural), that (feminine)
dieser - this (masculine)
Ding, das - thing
dort - there (place)
dort(hin) - there (direction)
draußen - outside
drei - three
dreihundert - three hundred
dreißig - thirty

dreizehn - thirteen
dritter - third
du, Sie - you
dunkel - dark
Dusche, die - shower
Ecke, die - corner
Ei, das - egg
ein - one
ein bisschen - a bit, a little
ein Stückchen - a little piece
(ein)giessen - to pour in
einen Job finden - to get a job
einen Vertrag schließen - enter into a contract
Eingang, der - entry, entrance
eingehen - to go into
einige - a few, some
einladen - to invite
Einpersonen- - single, with space for one person
einschalten - to turn on
Eis, das - ice cream
Eltern, die - parents
England - England
Engländerin, die - Englishwoman
Englisch - English
entgegen - towards
entlang - along
entscheiden - to decide
Entschluss, der; die Entscheidung - decision
er/sie/es - he/she/it
Erdbeere, die - strawberry

Erde, die; der Boden - earth, ground, soil

Erfahrung, die - experience

erklären - to explain

erreichen - to arrive, get to

erster - first

es gibt, es sind - there is, there are

essen - to eat; Essen, das - food

Etage, die - floor, storey

etwas - something

Euro, der - Euro

Fach, das; das Ding - subject, thing

fahren - to drive, to transport, to take by, to ride, to go

Fahrer, der - driver

Fahrkarte, die - ticket

Fahrt, die - passage; fare

Familie, die - family

Familien- - family (adj.)

Familienname, der - last name

Farbe, die - color

Fenster, das - window

Fernseher, der - tv-set

fertig - ready, prepared

Fertigkeit, die; die Kenntnis - skill

Film, der - film

finden - to find

Fisch, der - fish

Flasche, die - bottle

Fleisch- - meat (adj.)

fliegen - to fly

fließend - free(ly), fluently

Flug, der - flight

Flughafen, der - airport

Flugzeug, das - airplane

Flur, der - hall

Fluss, der - river

Formel, die - formula

Foto, das - photograph

fotografieren - to take photos/pictures

Fragebogen, der - questionnaire

fragen - to ask

Frank - Frank

Französisch - French (adj.)

Frau, die - woman

frei - free

Freitag, der - Friday

Freund, der - friend

Freundin, die - friend (female)

Frieden, der; die Welt - peace; world

früher - before, earlier

Frühstück, das - breakfast

frühstücken, Frühstück essen - to have breakfast

fühlen - to feel

führen, leiten - to lead, to drive

Führerschein - driving license

fünf - five

fünfzehn - fifteen

funkionieren - to act, to work

für - for

Fußball- - soccer (adj.); Fußball, der - soccer

Fußballspieler, der - soccer player

Fußboden, der; die Etage - floor

Gabel, die - fork

ganze, (die) - whole (feminine)
Garage, die - garage
Garten, der - garden
Gas- - gas (adj.)
Gast, der - guest
geben - to give
geboren sein - to be born
geeignet, passend - suitable, fitting
gefallen - to like, to appeal
gegenüber - across from
gehen - to go, to walk, to head
gelb - yellow
Geld, das - money
Geldtasche, die; das Portmonee - wallet
gelingen - to succeed, to go off well
Gemüse, das - vegetable
gemütlich - cozily/cozy, comfortable
genug sein; greifen - to be enough; to grab
Geographie, die; die Erdkunde - geography
Gepäck, das - baggage
geradeaus - straight
geräumig - spacious
Geschäft, das; der Laden - store, shop
Geschichte, die - history
Geschirr, das - dishes
gesellig - sociable
Getränk, das - drink
gießen - to pour (something fluid)
Glas, das - glass; Glas-, gläsern - glass (adj.)
grau - gray
greifen - to reach
Griff, der - handle

groß - big
Großbritannien - Great Britain
grün - green
Grünfläche, die - greenery
Gummi- - rubber (adj.)
Gurke, die - cucumber
gut - good, well
haben - to have, to own
Hälfte, die - half
Hallo - hi, hello
Haltestelle, die - stop
Hamburger, der - hamburger
Hand, die - hand
Handarbeit, die - physical work
Handtuch, das - towel
hängen - to hang
Haus, das - house; Haus-, häuslich - house/home (adj.)
Heft, das - notebook, copybook
heiß - hot
helfen - to help
hell - bright
(her)einkommen - to enter
herangehen, sich nähern - to approach
Herd, der - stove
herrlich - excellent
heute - today
hier - here
hier(her) - here (direction)
(hin)ausgehen - to go out, get out
(hin)zufügen - to add
hinbringen - to bring, to carry

hinter - behind, for
hoch - high
hölzern, Holz- - wooden
Honig, der - honey
hören - to listen to
Hörsaal, der - auditorium, class-room
Hotel, das - hotel
Hühnchen, das - chicken
Hühner, die - chickens
Hund, der - dog
ich - I
ihn, sein - him, his
ihr - your(s) (plural)
immer - always
Immobilie, die; das Grundbesitz - real estate
in - in, into
in der Mitte - in the middle
(in) Teilzeit - part-time
innen, drinnen - inside
interessant - interesting
irgendwann - sometime, some day
irgendwelcher - any, some
Italien - Italy
Italiener, der - Italian (person)
ja - yes
Jahr, das - year
Jahre - years
jeder - every
jemand - someone
jene(r/s) - that
jetzt - now
Kaffee, der - coffee

Kaffeemaschine, die - coffeemaker
kalt, kühl - cold
Kamin, der - fireplace
Karotte, die - carrot(s)
Käse, der - cheese
Kasse, die - checkout, cash register
Kasserolle, die; der (Koch)topf - saucepan
kassieren - to scan
Kassierer, der - cashier, teller
Katze, die - cat
kaufen - to buy
Keks, der; das Törtchen - cookie
Kellner, der - waiter
kennen - to know
kennenlernen - to get acquainted, to learn
Kind, das - child
Kinder- - children's (adj.), child (adj.)
Kinderkrippe - nursery
Kino, das - cinema, movie theater
Kiosk, der - kiosk
Kissen, das - pillow
Kleidung, die - clothing, robe
klein - small
Klingel, die - bell, ring
Klinik, die - clinic
klopfen - to knock
Klub, der - club
Kohl, der - cabbage
Komödie, die - comedy
können - to be able to, can
Korb, der - basket
kosten - to cost

krank sein - to be sick

krank werden, erkranken - to get sick

Kreide, die - chalk

Kronleuchter, der - chandelier

Küche, die - kitchen

Küchen- - kitchen (adj.)

kühl - cold

Kühlschrank, der - refrigerator

Kunststoff-, aus Kunststoff - plastic (adj.)

lachen - to laugh

Lachs, der - salmon

Lampe, die - lamp

(Land)karte, die - map

Land, das - country

lange - long, for a long time

Laptop, der - laptop

laufen - to run

Läufer, der; der Bettvorleger - little rug, mat

laut - noisily / noisy

leben - to live; Leben, das - life

Lebensmittel, die - products, food

Lebensmittelgeschäft, das - grocery (adj.)

lecker - tasty

ledern, Leder- - leather (adj.)

leer - empty

legen - to put (down)

Lehrbuch, das - textbook

lehren, beibringen - to teach

Lehrer, der - teacher, instructor

leicht - light; leicht - light (adj.)

Leiter, der; der Chef - manager, head

lernen - to study, to learn

lesen - to read

letztens, kürzlich - not long ago, recently

leuchten, scheinen - to shine

Leute, die - people

Licht, das - light

Liebe, die - love

lieben - to love

liegen - to lie

Lineal, das - ruler

links - on the left

Liter, der - liter

Löffel, der - spoon

Londoner - London (adj.)

lustig - funny

machen - do, carry out, to make; machen, schaffen - to do (finish)

Mädchen, das - girl

-mal (einmal, zweimal etc.) - time(s) (as in "how many times")

manchmal - sometimes

Mann, der - man

männlich - male

Maschine, die - machine

Mechaniker, der - mechanic

mehr, noch - more, still

mein - my (mine); mein, dein etc. (eigen) - someone's (own)

Messer, das - knife

metallen, Metall- - metal (adj.)

Mikrowelle, die - microwave

Milch- - dairy, milk (adj.); Milch, das - milk

Minibus, der - minibus

Minute, die - minute

mit - with
Mittagsessen, das - lunch
Mixer, der - mixer
Möbel, die - furniture
möglich - possible
Monat, der - month
morgen - tomorrow; Morgen, der - morning
Motorrad, das - motorcycle, motorbike
müde werden - to get tired
Müll, der; der Abfall - trash, garbage
Museum, das - museum
Mutter, die Mama - Mom
nach - after
nach Hause - homeward
Nachbar, der - neighbor
nächster - following, next
nah, in der Nähe - near
Name, der - name
national - national
Nationalität, die - nationality
natürlich - of course
Neapel - Naples
neben - next to, near
nehmen - to take (a shower, medicine etc.)
nein; es gibt kein(e/en) - no; there isn't, there aren't
neu - new
neun - nine
neunzehn - nineteen
nicht - not
nicht groß - not big, not tall
nicht neu - not new

nicht teuer, preisgünstig - inexpensive
nicht weit - not far
nie(mals) - never
Niederländer, der - Dutchman
niederländisch - Dutch (adj.)
normalerweise - normally, usually
notieren - to write down
nötig, notwendig - necessary
Nudeln, die - pasta, macaroni
Nummer, die - number
nur - only, just
ob - whether, if
ober - on top of, over, above
Oberleitungsbus, der; der Obus - trolleybus
Obst, das - fruit
oder - or
öffnen, aufmachen - to open
oft - often
ohne - without
Oma, die; die alte Frau - grandmother, old woman
Opa, der; der alte Mann - grandfather, old man
Orange, die - orange
Orangen- - orange (adj.)
Ort, der; der Platz - place
Ozean, der - ocean
Paar, das - pair
Päckchen, das - package
Paket, das - packet
Papa, der - Dad
Papier, das - paper

Park, der - park
Parzelle, die - area, site
Pass, der - passport
Pause, die - break
Periode, die - period
Person, die; der Mensch - person
persönlich - personal
Pfirsich, der - peach
Philip - Philip
Physik, die - physics
Pilz, der - mushroom
Pizza, die - pizza
(Platz) nehmen - to occupy
Platz, der - (city) square
Polizei, die - police
Polizist, der - policeman
Polyethylen- - polyethylene, plastic (adj.)
Postamt, das - post office
Preis, der; die Kosten (pl.) - value, price
professionell - professional
Prüfung, die - test
purpurrot - purple
Rechnung, die - bill, receipt
Rechte, die - rights
rechts - on the right
(Rechts)anwalt, der - lawyer
reden, sich unterhalten - to talk
Regal, das - shelf
Regel, die - rule
Regen, der - rain
reinigen, sauber machen - to clean
Reis, der - rice

reisen - to travel
Renovierung, die - renovation, repairs
Restaurant, das - restaurant
Richtung, die - direction
roh - raw
Rose, die - rose
rot - red
rufen, nennen - to call, to name
ruhig - calm(ly)
rund - round
(rund) um - around
Rundfunk, der; das Radio - radio
Saal, der; die Halle - hall, auditorium
Saft, der - juice
sagen - to tell
Sahne, die - sour cream
sammeln - to collect, to gather
Sammlung, die - collection
Samstag, der - Saturday
Sarah - Sarah
sauber - clean
Schachtel, die; die Kiste - box
Schalter, der - switch
Schiff, das - ship
Schlaf- - sleep (adj.)
Schlange, die - line, queue
Schlüssel, der - key
schmutzig - dirty
schneiden - to cut
schnell - quickly
schon - already
schön - pretty, beautiful

Schrank, der; das Regal - cupboard, wardrobe, bookcase

schrecklich, fürchterlich - scary

schreiben - to write

Schriftstellerin, die - writer (fem.)

Schublade, die - drawer, box

Schule, die - school

Schüler, der - student, pupil

schütten - to pour (something loose)

schwarz - black

schweigend - without speaking, silently

Schwester, die - sister

schwimmen - to swim

sechs - six

See, der - lake; See, die; das Meer - sea

sehen - to see

sehr - very

Seife, die - soap

sein - to be

Seite, die - page

(Selbstbedienungs)Wäscherei, die - laundromat, launderette

Serviette, die - napkin

Sessel, der - armchair

Shakespeare - Shakespeare

sich ankleiden - to get dressed

sich ausruhen, sich erholen - to rest, to relax

sich befinden - to be (located)

sich bemühen - to work hard

sich bewegen - to move

sich einrichten - to settle

sich erwärmen - to warm up

sich setzen - to sit down

sich verabreden - to arrange, to make an appointment

sich verabschieden - to say goodbye

sich versammeln - to gather together

sich vorbereiten - to prepare oneself

sich waschen - to wash oneself

sie (Pl.) - they; sie (Sing.) - her; sie, ihr (Pl.) - them, their(s)

sieben - seven

Sitz- - sitting

sitzen - to sit

so - like this, so

so dass - in order to, so that

Sofa, das - sofa, couch

sofort, auf der Stelle - right away

sollen - to have to, to be obliged

Sonne, die - sun

Sonntag, der - Sunday

sorgfältig - careful

Spanier, der - Spaniard

spazieren gehen - to take a walk

Speise, die; das Gericht - dish

Speisezimmer, das - dining room

Spiegel, der - mirror

Spiel, das - game

spielen - to play

Sprache, die; die Zunge - language, tongue

sprechen, plaudern - to talk, to chat, to speak

Springbrunnen, der; die Fontäne - fountain

Stadt, die - city

Stand, der - rack, stand; Stand, der; der Status - status

Station, die; der Bahnhof - station

Stau, der - traffic jam

stehen - to stand

stehlen - to steal

steigen - to go up, to ascend, to rise

stellen, legen - to put (vertically)

still, leise - quiet, quietly

Strand, der - beach

Straße, die - street

Stück, das - piece

Student, der - university student

Stuhl, der - chair

Stunde, die - hour

suchen - to search, to look for

Supermarkt, der - supermarket

Suppe, die - soup

süß - sweet

Tag, der - day

Tasche, die - purse, bag

Tasse, die - cup

Taxi, das - taxi

Technologie, die - technology

Tee, der - tea; Tee- - tea (adj.)

(Tee) kochen - to boil, to brew

Teekessel, der - teapot

Teilzeitarbeit, die - part-time job

Telefon, das - phone; Telefon- - telephone (adj.)

Teller, der - plate

Teppich, der - carpet

teuer - expensive

Theater, das - theater

Tier, das - animal

Tisch, der - table

Tischlein, das - caffee table, little table

Tischtuch, das - tablecloth

Toaster, der - toaster

Toilette, die - bathroom, toilet (bowl)

Toiletten- - toilet, bathroom (adj.)

Tomate, die - tomato

Tourist, der - tourist

tragen - to carry

Transport, der; der Verkehr - transport

Transportarbeiter, der; der Packer - loader, stevedore

Traube(n), die - grape(s)

treffen - to meet

(Treppen)Stufe, die - step

Treppenhaus, das - staircase

treten, trampeln - to trample

trinken - to drink

Trockner, der; der Fön (für die Haare) - drier

Tulpe, die - tulip

Tunnel, der - tunnel

Tür, die - door

U-Bahn, die - metro, subway

über - about, over, along; über, (z.B. eine Stunde) lang - through, in (time)

(über)kochen, sieden - to boil

Ufer, das - shore

umziehen - to move (to change address)

und - and

ungefähr - roughly, approximately

Universität, die - university

uns - us

unser - our(s)

unter - among, under

Unterkunft, die; die Wohnung - accomodation, apartment

Unterricht, das; die Kurse, die Fächer - classes

Urlaub, der; die Ferien - vacation

Vase, die - vase

Vater, der - father

verdienen - to earn

vergehen - to pass

verheiratet - married (for men)

verkaufen - to sell

verkauft werden - to be sold

verschieden - different, various

Versicherung, die - insurance

versprechen - to promise

Vertreter, der; der Agent - agent

viele - many, a lot

vielleicht - maybe

vier - four

vierter - fourth

vierzig - forty

Vogel, der - bird

voll - full

vom Anfang an - from the beginning

vorbei, neben - past, near

Vorort, der; die Vorstadt - suburb

Vorschlag, der - suggestion

vorschlagen - to suggest, to offer

Waage, die - scales

wachsen - to grow

Wagen, der - wagon, carriage, cart

wählen - to choose

wahrscheinlich - probably

Wand, die - wall

wann, als - when

warm - warm

warten - to wait

warum - why

was - what

Wasch- (z.B. Waschpulver) - laundry, washing (adj.)

Waschbecken, das - washbasin

Wäsche, die; die Unterwäsche - laundry, underwear, linen

waschen - to wash, launder, to clean; Waschen, das - washer, washing

Wasser, das - water

Wasserhahn, der - faucet, tap

(weg)nehmen - to pick up, to take away

Weg, der - path, way, road

wegfahren - to go/ride away

weich - soft

weil - because

weinen - to cry

weiß - white

weit - far (away), at a long distance

weiter - further

weitermachen - to continue

welche(r/s), was für ein(e) - which, what

welcher - which

wenig - little, few
wer - who
Werbung, die - commercial, advertisement
werden - to become
wessen - whose
Wetter, der - weather
wie - how; wie viele Jahre - how many years
wiegen - to weigh
wieviel - how much
wir - we
Wirt, der - owner
wo - where
Woche, die - week
woher - from where
wohin - where to
Wohnung, die - apartment, flat
Wohnzimmer, das - living room
wollen - to want
wünschen - to wish, to desire
Wurst, die - baloney, kielbasa, sausage
Zahn, der - tooth; Zahn- - tooth (adj.)
Zahnarzt, der - dentist
Zähne, die (Pl.) - teeth
zehn - ten
zeigen - to show
Zeit, die - time

Zeitschrift, die - magazine
Zeitung, die - newspaper
zentral - central
Zentrum, das - center
Zimmer, das - room
Zitrone, die - lemon
zu Fuß - on foot
zu Hause - at home
zu Mittag essen - to have lunch
zu, nach - to
zubereiten - to prepare, to cook
Zucker, der - sugar
Zug, der - train
zurück - back
zurückgeben, abgeben - to give in, return
zurückkehren - to return
zusammen, gemeinsam - together
Zusammenfassung, die; das Resümee - synopsis, outline
zustimmen - to agree
zwanzig - twenty
zwei - two
zweiter - second
zwischen - between
zwölf - twelve
zwölfter - twelfth

Wörterbuch Englisch-Deutsch

a bit, a little - ein bisschen

a few, some - einige

a little piece - ein Stückchen

about - über

accomodation, apartment - die Unterkunft, die Wohnung

accompany; to spend (time) - begleiten; verbringen

across from - gegenüber

act, to work - funkionieren

active - aktiv

add - (hin)zufügen

address - die Addresse

adventure - das Abenteuer

after - nach

afterwards, then - dann

age - das Alter

agency - die Agentur, das Büro

agent - der Vertreter, der Agent

agree - zustimmen

airplane - das Flugzeug

airport - der Flughafen

aisle (in a store), section - die Abteilung

alcoholic - Alkohol-

all - alles

along - entlang

already - schon

also, too - auch

always - immer

among - unter

and - und

animal - das Tier

announcement, ad - die Anzeige

answer - antworten

any, some - irgendwelcher

apartment, flat - die Wohnung

apple - der Apfel

approach - herangehen, sich nähern

area, site - die Parzelle

armchair - der Sessel

around - (rund) um

arrange, to make an appointment - sich verabreden

arrive, get to - erreichen

ask - fragen

at home - zu Hause

at, near - bei, an

auditorium, class-room - der Hörsaal

automobile, car - das Auto, der Wagen; automobile (adj.) - Auto-

back - zurück

baggage - das Gepäck

baloney, kielbasa, sausage - die Wurst

banana - die Banane

bank - die Bank; bank (adjective) - Bank-

bar - die Bar, die Gaststätte

basket - der Korb

basketball - der Basketball

bathroom - das Badezimmer, das Bad, die Toilette

bathtub - die Badewanne

be - sein

be (located) - sich befinden

be able to, can - können

be born - geboren sein

be enough; to grab - genug sein; greifen

be left, to stay - bleiben

be necessary, to need to - brauchen

be sick - krank sein

be sold - verkauft werden

beach - der Strand

because - weil

become - werden

bed - das Bett

before, earlier - früher

beginning - der Anfang

behind, for - hinter

beige - beigefarben, beige (unflektiert), sandfarbig

bell, ring - die Klingel

better - besser

between - zwischen

big - groß

bill - die Rechnung

biology - die Biologie

bird - der Vogel

black - schwarz

blender - der Blender

blue - blau

board - das Brett

boil - (über)kochen, sieden; boil, to brew - (Tee) kochen

book - das Buch; book (adj.) - Buch-

bottle - die Flasche

boulevard - der Boulevard

box - die Schachtel, die Kiste

bread - das Brot

breadroll, bun - das Brötchen

break - die Pause

breakfast - das Frühstück

bridge - die Brücke

bright - hell

bring, to carry - hinbringen

brother - der Bruder

brown - braun

brush - die Bürste

Brussels - Brüssel

burn - brennen

bus - der Bus; bus (adj.) - Bus-

busy - beschäftigt

but, while, and - aber, doch, und

buy - kaufen

cabbage - der Kohl

cafe - das Café

caffee table - das Tischlein

cake, dessert - das Dessert, der Nachtisch

call, to name - rufen, nennen; call (by phone) - anrufen

calm(ly) - ruhig

car service - der Autoservice

careful - sorgfältig

carefully, attentively - aufmerksam

carpet - der Teppich

carrot(s) - die Karotte

carry - tragen

cash - das Bargeld
cashier, teller - der Kassierer
cat - die Katze
ceiling - die Decke
center - das Zentrum
central - zentral
chair - der Stuhl
chalk - die Kreide
chandelier - der Kronleuchter
checkout, cash register - die Kasse
cheese - der Käse
chicken - das Hühnchen
chickens - die Hühner
child - das Kind
children's (adj.), child (adj.) - Kinder-
choose - wählen
cinema, movie theater - das Kino
city - die Stadt
(city) square - der Platz
classes - das Unterricht, der Unterricht, die Kurse, die Fächer
clean - reinigen, sauber, sauber machen; clean, to tidy up - aufräumen
clinic - die Klinik
clothing, robe - die Kleidung
club - der Klub
coffee - der Kaffee
coffeemaker - die Kaffeemaschine
cold - kalt, kühl
collect, to gather - sammeln
collection - die Sammlung
color - die Farbe

comedy - die Komödie
comfortable - bequem
commercial, advertisement - die Werbung
computer - der Computer
consultant - der Berater
continue - weitermachen
cookie - der Keks, das Törtchen
corner - die Ecke
cost - kosten
country - das Land
cozily - gemütlich
cozy, comfortable - gemütlich
cry - weinen
cucumber - die Gurke
cup - die Tasse
cupboard, wardrobe, bookcase - der Schrank, das Regal
cut - schneiden
cut off - abschneiden
Dad - der Papa
dairy, milk (adj.) - Milch-
dark - dunkel
data, information - die Angaben
day - der Tag
dean's office - das Dekanat
decide - entscheiden
decision - der Entschluss, die Entscheidung
dentist - der Zahnarzt
design - das Design
detective - der Detektiv
different, various - verschieden
dining room - das Speisezimmer

direction - die Richtung

dirty - schmutzig

discuss - besprechen

dish - die Speise, das Gericht

dishes - das Geschirr

display, to set out - auslegen

do (finish), carry out - machen, schaffen

doctor, physician - der Arzt

dog - der Hund

door - die Tür

drawer, box - die Schublade

drier - der Trockner, der Fön (für die Haare)

drink - das Getränk, trinken

drive out - ausfahren

drive, to transport - fahren

driver - der Fahrer

driving license - Führerschein

drugstore - die Apotheke

Dutch (adj.) - niederländisch

Dutchman - der Niederländer

earn - verdienen

earth, ground, soil - die Erde, der Boden

eat - essen

education - die Ausbildung, die Erziehung

egg - das Ei

eight - acht

eight hundred - achthundert

eighteen - achtzehn

elevator - der Aufzug

employment, job - die Anstellung, die Beschäftigung

empty - leer

England - England

English - Englisch

Englishwoman - die Engländerin

enter - (her)einkommen

enter into a contract - einen Vertrag schließen

entry, entrance - der Eingang

Euro - der Euro

evening - der Abend

every - jeder

everything - alles

excellent - herrlich

exit - der Ausgang

expensive - teuer

experience - die Erfahrung

explain - erklären

family - die Familie; family (adj.) - Familien-

far (away), at a long distance - weit

father - der Vater

faucet, tap - der Wasserhahn

feel - fühlen

fifteen - fünfzehn

fill out - ausfüllen

filled out - ausgefüllt

film - der Film

find - finden

fireplace - der Kamin

first - erster

fish - der Fisch

five - fünf

flakes, cereal - die Cerealien

flight - der Flug

floor, storey - der Fußboden, die Etage

flower - die Blume

fly - fliegen

following, next - nächster

food - das Essen

for - für

fork - die Gabel

formula - die Formel

forty - vierzig

fountain - der Springbrunnen, die Fontäne

four - vier

fourth - vierter

Frank - Frank

free - frei

free(ly), fluently - fließend

French (adj.) - Französisch

Friday - der Freitag

friend - der Freund; friend (female) - die Freundin

from the beginning - vom Anfang an

from where - woher

from, out of - aus, von

fruit - das Obst

full - voll

funny - lustig

furniture - die Möbel

further - weiter

game - das Spiel

garage - die Garage

garden - der Garten

gas (adj.) - Gas-

gather together - sich versammeln

geography - die Geographie, die Erdkunde

German - Deutsch

get (something) - bekommen

get a job - einen Job finden

get acquainted, to learn - kennenlernen

get dressed - sich ankleiden

get sick - krank werden, erkranken

get tired - müde werden

get treated - behandelt werden

get up - aufstehen

get, to reach, to take something out - bekommen, nach etwas greifen

girl - das Mädchen

give - geben

give in, return - zurückgeben, abgeben

glass - das Glas; glass (adj.) - Glas-, gläsern

glasses - die Brille

go into - eingehen

go out, get out - (hin)ausgehen

go up, to ascend, to rise - steigen

go, to walk - gehen

go/ride away - wegfahren

good - gut

grandfather, old man - der Opa, der alte Mann

grandmother, old woman - die Oma, die alte Frau

grape(s) - die Traube(n)

gray - grau

Great Britain - Großbritannien

green - grün

greenery - die Grünfläche

grocery (adj.) - das Lebensmittelgeschäft

grow - wachsen
guest - der Gast
half - die Hälfte
hall - der Flur; hall, auditorium - der Saal, die Halle
hamburger - der Hamburger
hand - die Hand
handle - der Griff
hang - hängen
have breakfast - frühstücken, Frühstück essen
have lunch - zu Mittag essen
have to, to be obliged - sollen
have, to own - haben
he/she/it - er/sie/es
head - gehen
hello - Hallo
help - helfen
her - sie (Sing.)
here (direction) - hier(her)
hi, hello - Hallo
high - hoch
highway - die Autobahn
hill, mountain - der Berg
him, his - ihn, sein
history - die Geschichte
homeward - nach Hause
honey - der Honig
hot - heiß
hotel - das Hotel
hour - die Stunde
house - das Haus

house/home (adj.) - Haus-, häuslich
how - wie
how many years - wie viele Jahre
how much - wieviel
I - ich
ice cream - das Eis
in English - auf Englisch
in French - auf Französisch
in German - auf Deutsch
in order to, so that - so dass
in Spanish - auf Spanisch
in the evening - abends, am Abend
in the middle - in der Mitte
in, into - in
indicate - anzeigen, andeuten
indicated - angezeigt
inexpensive - nicht teuer, preisgünstig
information (adj.), referential (adj.) - Auskunfts-
inside - innen, drinnen
insurance - die Versicherung
interesting - interessant
invite - einladen
Italian (person) - der Italiener
Italy - Italien
juice - der Saft
key - der Schlüssel
kiosk - der Kiosk
kitchen - die Küche; kitchen (adj.) - Küchen-
knife - das Messer
knock - klopfen
know - kennen

lake - der See

lamp - die Lampe

language, tongue - die Sprache, die Zunge

laptop - der Laptop

last name - der Familienname

laugh - lachen

laundromat, launderette - die (Selbstbedienungs)Wäscherei

laundry, underwear, linen - die Wäsche, die Unterwäsche

laundry, washing (adj.) - Wasch- (z.B. Waschpulver)

lawyer - der (Rechts)anwalt

lead, to drive - führen, leiten

leather (adj.) - ledern, Leder-

lemon - die Zitrone

librarian - der Bibliothekar

library - die Bibliothek, die Bücherei

lie - liegen

life - das Leben

light - das Licht, leicht; light (adj.) - leicht

like this, so - so

like, to appeal - gefallen

line, queue - die Schlange

listen to - hören

liter - der Liter

little rug, mat - der Läufer, der Bettvorleger

little table - das Tischlein

little, few - wenig

live - leben

living room - das Wohnzimmer

loader, stevedore - der Transportarbeiter, der Packer

long, for a long time - lange

look (like) - aussehen

love - die Liebe, lieben

lunch - das Mittagsessen

machine - die Maschine

magazine - die Zeitschrift

make - machen

male - männlich

man - der Mann

manager, head - der Leiter, der Chef

many, a lot - viele

map - die (Land)karte

married (for men) - verheiratet

maybe - vielleicht

meat (adj.) - Fleisch-

mechanic - der Mechaniker

meet - treffen

memorial, monument - das Denkmal

metal (adj.) - metallen, Metall-

metro, subway - die U-Bahn

microwave - die Mikrowelle

milk - das Milch

minibus - der Minibus

minute - die Minute

mirror - der Spiegel

mixer - der Mixer

Mom - die Mutter, Mama

money - das Geld

month - der Monat

more, still - mehr, noch

morning - der Morgen

motorcycle, motorbike - das Motorrad

move - sich bewegen; move (to change address) - umziehen
museum - das Museum
mushroom - der Pilz
my (mine) - mein
name - der Name
napkin - die Serviette
Naples - Neapel
national - national
nationality - die Nationalität
near - nah, in der Nähe
necessary - nötig, notwendig
neighbor - der Nachbar
never - nie(mals)
new - neu
newspaper - die Zeitung
next to, near - neben
nine - neun
nineteen - neunzehn
no; there isn't, there aren't - nein; es gibt kein(e/en)
noisily / noisy - laut
normally, usually - normalerweise
not - nicht
not big - nicht groß
not far - nicht weit
not long ago, recently - letztens, kürzlich
not new - nicht neu
not tall - nicht groß
notebook, copybook - das Heft
now - jetzt
number - die Nummer

nursery - Kinderkrippe
occupy - (Platz) nehmen
ocean - der Ozean
of course - natürlich
office - das Büro
often - oft
old - alt
older - älter
on - auf
on foot - zu Fuß
on the left - links
on the right - rechts
on top of, over, above - ober
one - ein
one and a half - anderthalb
only, just - nur
open - öffnen, aufmachen
or - oder
orange - die Orange; orange (adj.) - Orangen-
order - bestellen
other - andere(r/s)
our(s) - unser
outside - draußen
over, along - über
owner - der Wirt
package - das Päckchen
packet - das Paket
page - die Seite
pair - das Paar
paper - das Papier
parents - die Eltern

park - der Park
part-time - (in) Teilzeit
part-time job - die Teilzeitarbeit
pass - vergehen
passage; fare - die Fahrt
passport - der Pass
past, near - vorbei, neben
pasta, macaroni - die Nudeln
path, way - der Weg
pay - (be)zahlen
peace; world - der Frieden; die Welt
peach - der Pfirsich
pencil - der Bleistift
people - die Leute
period - die Periode
person - die Person, der Mensch
personal - persönlich
phone - das Telefon
photograph - das Foto
physical work - die Handarbeit
physics - die Physik
pick up, to take away - (weg)nehmen
picture - das Bild
piece - das Stück
pillow - das Kissen
pineapple - die Ananas
pizza - die Pizza
place - der Ort, der Platz
placement, employment - die Anstellung
plastic (adj.) - Kunststoff-, aus Kunststoff
plate - der Teller
play - spielen

police - die Polizei
policeman - der Polizist
polyethylene, plastic (adj.) - Polyethylen-
possible - möglich
post office - das Postamt
(potato) chips - die Chips
pour (something fluid) - gießen; pour (something loose) - schütten
pour in - (ein)giessen
prepare oneself - sich vorbereiten
prepare, to cook - zubereiten
pretty, beautiful - schön
price - der Preis
probably - wahrscheinlich
products, food - die Lebensmittel
profession - der Beruf, das Fach
professional - professionell
promise - versprechen
purple - purpurrot
purse, bag - die Tasche
put (down) - legen; put (vertically) - stellen, legen
put on - anziehen
questionnaire - der Fragebogen
quickly - schnell
quiet - still
quietly - still, leise
rack, stand - der Stand
radio - der Rundfunk, das Radio
rain - der Regen
raw - roh
reach - greifen

read - lesen
ready, prepared - fertig
real estate - die Immobilie, das Grundbesitz
receipt - die Rechnung
red - rot
refrigerator - der Kühlschrank
refuse - ablehnen, absagen
renovation, repairs - die Renovierung
rest, to relax - sich ausruhen, sich erholen
restaurant - das Restaurant
return - zurückgeben, zurückkehren
rice - der Reis
ride, to go - fahren
right away - sofort, auf der Stelle
rights - die Rechte
river - der Fluss
road - der Weg
roof - das Dach
room - das Zimmer
rose - die Rose
roughly, approximately - ungefähr
round - rund
rubber (adj.) - Gummi-
rule - die Regel
ruler - das Lineal
run - laufen
salmon - der Lachs
sandwich - das belegte Brot, die Schnitte
Sarah - Sarah
Saturday - der Samstag
saucepan - die Kasserolle, der (Koch)topf
sausage - die Wurst

say goodbye - sich verabschieden
scales - die Waage
scan - kassieren
scary - schrecklich, fürchterlich
school - die Schule
sea - die See, das Meer
search, to look for - suchen
second - zweiter
see - sehen
sell - verkaufen
settle - sich einrichten
seven - sieben
Shakespeare - Shakespeare
shelf - das Regal
shine - leuchten, scheinen
ship - das Schiff
shore - das Ufer
show - zeigen
shower - die Dusche
sidewalk - der Bürgersteig, der Fußweg
single, with space for one person - Einpersonen-
sink - der Ausguss, das Becken
sister - die Schwester
sit - sitzen
sit down - sich setzen
sitting - Sitz-
six - sechs
skill - die Fertigkeit, die Kenntnis
sleep (adj.) - Schlaf-
small - klein
so, because of this - deshalb

soap - die Seife

soccer - der Fußball; soccer (adj.) - Fußball-

soccer player - der Fußballspieler

sociable - gesellig

sofa, couch - das Sofa

soft - weich

someone - jemand

someone's (own) - mein, dein etc. (eigen)

something - etwas

sometime, some day - irgendwann

sometimes - manchmal

soon - bald

soup - die Suppe

sour cream - die Sahne

spacious - geräumig

Spaniard - der Spanier

speak - sprechen

spoon - der Löffel

staircase - das Treppenhaus

stamp - die Briefmarke

stand - stehen

start - anfangen, beginnen

station - die Station, der Bahnhof

status - der Stand, der Status

steal - stehlen

step - die (Treppen)Stufe

stop - die Haltestelle

store, shop - das Geschäft, der Laden

stove - der Herd

straight - geradeaus

strawberry - die Erdbeere

street - die Straße

student, pupil - der Schüler

study, to learn - lernen

subject, thing - das Fach; das Ding

suburb - der Vorort, die Vorstadt

succeed, to go off well - gelingen

sugar - der Zucker

suggest, to offer - anbieten, vorschlagen

suggestion - der Vorschlag

suitable, fitting - geeignet, passend

sun - die Sonne

Sunday - der Sonntag

supermarket - der Supermarkt

sweet - süß

swim - schwimmen

switch - der Schalter

synopsis, outline - die Zusammenfassung, das Resümee

table - der Tisch

tablecloth - das Tischtuch

take (a shower, medicine etc.) - nehmen; take (time), to last - dauern

take a walk - spazieren gehen

take by, to drive, to transport - fahren

take photos/pictures - fotografieren

talk - reden, sich unterhalten; talk, to chat - sprechen, plaudern

tasty - lecker

taxi - das Taxi

tea - der Tee; tea (adj.) - Tee-

teach - lehren, beibringen

teacher, instructor - der Lehrer

teapot - der Teekessel

technology - die Technologie

teeth - die Zähne (Pl.)

telephone (adj.) - Telefon-

tell - sagen

ten - zehn

test - die Prüfung

textbook - das Lehrbuch

thanks - danke

that - jene(r/s); that (feminine) - diese (Sing.)

theater - das Theater

them, their(s) - sie, ihr (Pl.)

then, later - damals, dann

there (direction) - dort(hin); there (place) - dort

there is, there are - es gibt, es sind

these (plural) - diese (Pl.)

they - sie (Pl.)

thing - das Ding

think - denken

third - dritter

thirteen - dreizehn

thirty - dreißig

this - das; this (feminine) - diese (Fem.); this (masculine) - dieser

three - drei

three hundred - dreihundert

through, in (time) - über, (z.B. eine Stunde) lang

ticket - die Fahrkarte

time - die Zeit

time(s) (as in "how many times") - -mal (einmal, zweimal etc.)

to - zu, nach

toaster - der Toaster

today - heute

together - zusammen, gemeinsam

toilet (bowl) - die Toilette; toilet, bathroom (adj.) - Toiletten-

tomato - die Tomate

tomorrow - morgen

tooth - der Zahn; tooth (adj.) - Zahn-

tourist - der Tourist

towards - entgegen

towel - das Handtuch

traffic jam - der Stau

traffic lights - die Ampel

train - der Zug

trample - treten, trampeln

transport - der Transport, der Verkehr

trash, garbage - der Müll, der Abfall

travel - reisen

treatment - die Behandlung

tree - der Baum

trolleybus - der Oberleitungsbus, der Obus

tulip - die Tulpe

tunnel - der Tunnel

turn on - einschalten

tv-set - der Fernseher

twelfth - zwölfter

twelve - zwölf

twenty - zwanzig

two - zwei

under - unter

university - die Universität

university student - der Student

until, to - bis

us - uns

vacation - der Urlaub, die Ferien

value, price - der Preis, die Kosten (pl.)

vase - die Vase

vegetable - das Gemüse

very - sehr

wagon, carriage, cart - der Wagen

wait - warten

waiter - der Kellner

wake up - aufstehen

walk, to go - gehen

wall - die Wand

wallet - die Geldtasche, das Portmonee

want - wollen

warm - warm

warm (up) - aufwärmen; warm up - sich erwärmen

wash oneself - sich waschen

wash, launder, to clean - waschen

washbasin - das Waschbecken

washer, washing - das Waschen

watch - anschauen

water - das Wasser

we - wir

weather - der Wetter

week - die Woche

weigh - wiegen

well - gut

what - was

when - wann, als

where - wo

where to - wohin

whether, if - ob

which, what - welche(r/s), was für ein(e)

white - weiß

who - wer

whole (feminine) - (die) ganze

whose - wessen

why - warum

window - das Fenster

wish, to desire - wünschen

with - mit

without - ohne

without speaking, silently - schweigend

woman - die Frau

wooden - hölzern, Holz-

work - die Arbeit; work (adj.) - Arbeits-; work, function - arbeiten, funktionieren

work hard - sich bemühen

worker - der Arbeiter

write - schreiben

write (down) - aufschreiben; write down - notieren

write out (a check) - ausschreiben

writer (fem.) - die Schriftstellerin

year - das Jahr

years - Jahre

yellow - gelb

yes - ja

you - du, Sie

your(s) - dein; your(s) (plural) - ihr

Starke Verben

Infinitiv	Präteritum	Perfekt (Past Participle)
anfangen begin	fing an began	angefangen begun
ankommen arrive	kam an arrived	ist angekommen arrived
anrufen call up	rief an called up	angerufen called up
backen bake	backte baked	gebacken baked
befehlen command	befahl commanded	befohlen commanded
beginnen begin	begann began	begonnen begun
beißen bite	biss bit	gebissen bitten
bekommen get, receive	bekam got	bekommen gotten
bergen salvage	barg salvaged	geborgen salvaged
bersten burst	barst burst	geborsten burst
betrügen deceive	betrog deceived	betrogen deceived
biegen bend	bog bent	gebogen bent
bieten offer	bot offered	geboten offered
binden tie	band tied	gebunden tied
bitten request	bat requested	gebeten requested
blasen blow	blies blew	geblasen blown
bleiben stay	blieb stayed	ist geblieben stayed
bleichen bleach	blich bleached	geblichen bleached
braten roast	briet roasted	gebraten roasted
brechen break	brach broke	gebrochen broken
brennen burn	brannte burned	gebrannt burned
bringen bring	brachte brought	gebracht brought
denken think	dachte thought	gedacht thought
dreschen thresh	drosch threshed	gedroschen threshed
dringen force	drang forced	gedrungen forced
dürfen may	durfte was allowed	gedurft been allowed
empfangen receive	empfing received	empfangen received
empfehlen recommend	empfahl recommended	empfohlen recommended
erfinden invent	erfand invented	erfunden invented

erlöschen extinguish	erlosch extinguished	erloschen extinguished
erschallen echo, sound	erscholl sounded	erschollen sounded
erschrecken scare	erschrak scared	erschrocken scared
essen eat	aß ate	gegessen eaten
fahren travel	fuhr traveled	ist gefahren traveled
fallen fall	fiel fell	ist gefallen fallen
fangen catch	fing caught	gefangen caught
fechten fence	focht fenced	gefochten fenced
finden find	fand found	gefunden found
fliegen fly	flog flew	ist geflogen flown
fliehen flee	floh fled	ist geflohen fled
fließen flow	floss flowed	ist geflossen flowed
fressen gorge	fraß gorged	gefressen gorged
frieren freeze	fror froze	gefroren frozen
frohlocken rejoice	frohlockte rejoiced	frohlockt rejoiced
gären ferment	gor fermented	gegoren fermented
gebären bear (child)	gebar bore	geboren born
geben give	gab gave	gegeben given
gedeihen flourish	gedieh flourished	ist gediehen flourished
gefallen be pleasing, like	gefiel liked	gefallen liked
gehen go	ging went	ist gegangen gone
gelingen succeed	gelang succeeded	ist gelungen succeeded
gelten be valid	galt was valid	gegolten been valid
genesen recover	genas recovered	genesen recovered
genießen enjoy	genoß enjoyed	genossen enjoyed
geschehen happen	geschah happened	ist geschehen happened
gewinnen win	gewann won	gewonnen won
gießen pour	goß poured	gegossen poured
gleichen resemble	glich resembled	geglichen resembled
gleiten glide, slide	glitt glided	ist geglitten glided
glimmen glow, smoulder	glomm glowed	ist geglommen glowed

graben dig	grub dug	gegraben dug
greifen grasp	griff grasped	gegriffen grasped
haben have	hatte had	gehabt had
halten hold	hielt held	gehalten held
hängen hang	hing hung/hanged	gehangen hung/hanged
hauen hew, hit	haute hit	gehauen hit
heben lift	hob lifted	gehoben lifted
heißen be called	hieß named	geheißen named
helfen help	half helped	geholfen helped
kennen know	kannte knew	gekannt known
klingen ring	klang rang	geklungen rung
kneifen pinch	kniff pinched	gekniffen pinched
kommen come	kam came	ist gekommen come
können can	konnte could	gekonnt could
kriechen crawl	kroch crawled	ist gekrochen crawled
laden load	lud loaded	geladen loaded
lassen let, allow	ließ let	gelassen let
laufen run	lief ran	ist gelaufen run
leiden suffer	litt suffered	gelitten suffered
leihen lend	lieh lent	geliehen lent
lesen read	las read	gelesen read
liegen lie	lag lay	gelegen lain
lügen lie	log lied	gelogen lied
mahlen grind	mahlte ground	gemahlen ground
meiden avoid	mied avoided	gemieden avoided
messen measure	maß measured	gemessen measured
misslingen fail	misslang failed	misslungen failed
mögen like	mochte liked	gemocht liked
müssen must	musste had to	gemusst had to
nehmen take	nahm took	genommen taken
nennen name	nannte named	genannt named

pfeifen whistle	pfiff whistled	gepfiffen whistled
preisen praise	pries praised	gepriesen praised
quellen gush	quoll gushed	ist gequollen gushed
raten advise	riet advised	geraten advised
reiben rub	rieb rubbed	gerieben rubbed
reißen tear	riss tore	gerissen torn
reiten ride	ritt rode	ist geritten ridden
rennen run	rannte ran	ist gerannt run
riechen smell	roch smelled	gerochen smelled
ringen wring	rang wrung	gerungen wrung
rinnen flow	rann flowed	ist geronnen flowed
rufen call	rief called	gerufen called
salzen salt	salzte salted	gesalzen/gesalzt salted
saufen drink	soff drank	gesoffen drunk
saugen suck	sog sucked	gesogen sucked
schaffen create; accomplish, make	schuf created	geschaffen created
scheiden depart; separate	schied separated	geschieden separated
scheinen shine	schien shone	geschienen shone
scheißen shit	schiss shit	geschissen shit
schelten scold	schalt scolded	gescholten scolded
schießen shoot	schoss shot	geschossen shot
schlafen sleep	schlief slept	geschlafen slept
schlagen hit	schlug hit	geschlagen hit
schleichen sneak	schlich sneaked	ist geschlichen sneaked
schleifen polish	schliff polished	geschliffen polished
schleißen slit	schliß slit	geschlissen slit
schließen close, lock	schloss closed	geschlossen closed
schlingen gulp (down)	schlang gulped	geschlungen gulped
schmeißen fling, toss	schmiss flung	geschmissen flung
schmelzen melt	schmolz melted	geschmolzen melted
schneiden cut	schnitt cut	geschnitten cut

schrecken scare	schrak/schreckte scared	geschreckt/geschrocken scared
schreiben write	schrieb wrote	geschrieben written
schreien scream	schrie screamed	geschrien screamed
schreiten step	schritt stepped	ist geschritten stepped
schweigen be silent	schwieg was silent	geschwiegen been silent
schwellen swell, rise	schwoll swelled	ist geschwollen swollen
schwimmen swim	schwamm swam	ist geschwommen swum
schwinden dwindle	schwand dwindled	ist geschwunden dwindled
schwingen swing	schwang swung	geschwungen swung
schwören swear	schwur/schwor swore	geschworen sworn
sehen see	sah saw	gesehen seen
sein be	war was	ist gewesen been
senden send, transmit	sandte sent	gesandt sent
sieden boil	sott/siedete boiled	gesotten boiled
singen sing	sang sang	gesungen sung
sinken sink	sank sank	ist gesunken sunk
sitzen sit	saß sat	gesessen sat
sollen should, ought to	sollte should	gesollt should
spalten split	spaltete split	gespalten/gespaltet split
speien spew	spie spewed	gespien spewed
spinnen spin	spann spun	gesponnen spun
sprechen speak	sprach spoke	gesprochen spoken
sprießen sprout	spross sprouted	gesprossen sprouted
springen jump	sprang jumped	ist gesprungen jumped
stechen stab, sting	stach stung	gestochen stung
stehen stand	stand stood	gestanden stood
stehlen steal	stahl stole	gestohlen stolen
steigen climb	stieg climbed	ist gestiegen climbed
sterben die	starb died	ist gestorben died
stieben fly about	stob flew about	ist gestoben flown about
stinken stink	stank stank	gestunken stunk

stoßen push, bump	stieß pushed	gestoßen pushed
streichen strike, paint	strich struck	gestrichen struck
streiten argue	stritt argued	gestritten argued
tragen carry, wear	trug wore	getragen worn
treffen meet	traf met	getroffen met
treiben move, drive	trieb drove	getrieben driven
triefen drip	triefte/troff dripped	getrieft dripped
trinken drink	trank drank	getrunken drunk
trügen be deceptive	trog was deceptive	getrogen been deceptive
tun do	tat did	getan done
überwinden overcome	überwand overcame	überwunden overcome
verderben spoil	verdarb spoiled	verdorben spoiled
verdrießen annoy	verdross annoyed	verdrossen annoyed
vergessen forget	vergaß forgot	vergessen forgotten
verlieren lose	verlor lost	verloren lost
verschleißen wear (out)	verschliss wore (out)	verschlissen worn (out)
verzeihen forgive	verzieh forgave	verziehen forgiven
wachsen grow	wuchs grew	ist gewachsen grown
waschsen wash	wusch washed	gewaschsen washed
weben weave	wob/webte wove	gewoben/gewebt woven
weichen yield	wich yielded	ist gewichen yielded
weisen indicate	wies indicated	gewiesen indicated
wenden turn	wandte turned	gewandt turned
werben recruit	warb recruited	geworben recruited
werden become	wurde became	ist geworden become
werfen throw	warf threw	geworfen thrown
wiegen weigh	wog/wiegte weighed	gewogen/gewiegt weighed
winden twist	wand twisted	gewunden twisted
wissen know	wusste knew	gewusst known
wollen want to	wollte wanted to	gewollt wanted to
wringen wring	wrang wrung	gewrungen wrung

zeihen accuse   zieh accused   geziehen accused
ziehen pull   zog pulled   gezogen pulled
zwingen compel   zwang compelled   gezwungen compelled

Wichtige Adjektive
Important adjectives

ängstlich - anxious
anständig - respectable, decent
anziehend - attractive
ärgerlich - annoying
aufgeregt - excited
ausgezeichnet - excellent
bescheiden - modest
bezaubernd - charming
böse - wicked, evil
dankbar - grateful, thankful
dumm - stupid
ehrgeizig - ambitious
ehrlich - honest
eifersüchtig - jealous
eifrig - eager
einfach - plain
entschlossen - resolute
erfahren - experienced
erfolgreich - successful
ernst - serious, grave
fleißig - diligent
frech - impudent
freundlich - friendly
froh - glad
geistreich - brilliant
geizig - mean

gemäßigt - moderate
gierig - greedy
gleichgütig - indifferent
glücklich - happy, lucky
grob - coarse, rude
häßlich - ugly
heftig - violent
hervorragend - excellent
hilflos - helpless
hilfsbereit - helpful
höflich - polite
hübsch - pretty, nice
jugendlich - youthful
klug - intelligent
lächerlich - ridiculous
langsam - slow
langweilig - boring
liebevoll - loving, affectionate
lustig - cheerful, merry, gay
mitfühlend - sympathetic
müde - tired
nervös - nervous
nett - nice, kind
neugierig - curious
oberflächlich - superficial, shallow
offen - frank, candid

pünktlich - punctual
rein - pure, clean
ruhig - calm, quiet, silent
schlau - cunning
schnell - fast
schön - beautiful
schüchtern - shy
schwach - weak
seltsam - strange, odd
sorgfältig - careful
spaßig - funny
traurig - sad
treu - faithful

überrascht - surprised
undankbar - ungrateful
ungebildet - uneducated
ungerecht - unjust, unfair
unglücklich - unhappy
verrückt - mad, crazy
vorsichtig - careful, prudent
weich - soft
weise - wise
wütend - furious
zäh - stubborn, tough
zufrieden - content
zuverlässig - reliable

Körperliche Eigenschaften

Physical qualities

groß - big
klein - small oder little
schnell - fast
langsam - slow
gut - good
schlecht - bad
teuer - expensive
billig - cheap
dick - thick
dünn - thin
eng - narrow
breit - wide
breit - broad
laut - loud
leise - quiet
intelligent - intelligent

dumm - stupid
nass - wet
trocken - dry
schwer - heavy
leicht - light
hart - hard
weich - soft
flach, seicht - shallow
tief - deep
leicht - easy
schwierig - difficult
schwach - weak
stark - strong
reich - rich
arm - poor
jung - young

alt - old
lang - long
kurz - short
hoch - high
tief - low
großzügig - generous
geizig - mean
richtig - true

falsch - false
schön - beautiful
hässlich - ugly
neu - new
alt - old
fröhlich, glücklich - happy
traurig - sad

Gegenteile
Antonyms

sicher - safe
gefährlich - dangerous
früh - early
spät - late
hell - light
dunkel - dark
offen, geöffnet - open
geschlossen, zu - closed oder shut
stramm, fest - tight
locker - loose
voll - full
leer - empty
viele - many
wenige - few
lebendig - alive
tot - dead
heiß - hot
kalt - cold
interessant - interesting
langweilig - boring

glücklich - lucky
unglücklich - unlucky
wichtig - important
unwichtig - unimportant
richtig - right
falsch - wrong
weit - far
nah - near
sauber - clean
schmutzig - dirty
nett - nice
gemein - nasty
angenehm - pleasant
unangenehm - unpleasant
ausgezeichnet - excellent
schrecklich - terrible
fair - fair
unfair - unfair
normal - normal
anormal - abnormal

List of the most common words

Tage der Woche	**Days of the week**
Der Sonntag	Sunday
Der Montag	Monday
Der Dienstag	Tuesday
Der Mittwoch	Wednesday
Der Donnerstag	Thursday
Der Freitag	Friday
Der Samstag	Saturday
Die Woche	week
Der Tag	day
Die Nacht	night
heute	today
gestern	yesterday
morgen	tomorrow
Der Morgen	morning
Der Abend	evening

Die Monate	**Months**
Der Januar	January
Der Februar	February
Der März	March
Der April	April
Der Mai	May
Der Juni	June
Der Juli	July
Der August	August
Der September	September
Der Oktober	October
Der November	November
Der Dezember	December

Die Jahreszeiten	**Seasons of the year**
Der Winter	winter
Der Frühling	spring
Der Sommer	summer
Der Herbst	autumn

Die Familie	**Family**
Die Tante	aunt
Der Bruder	brother
Die Kinder	children
Der Papa	dad
Die Tochter	daughter
Die Familie	family
Der Vater	father
Die Enkelin	granddaughter
Der Großvater	grandfather
Die Oma	grandmother
Die Großeltern	grandparents
Der Enkel	grandson
Der Urgroßvater	great-grandfather
Die Urgroßmutter	great-grandmother
Die Mutter	mother
Der Neffe	nephew
Die Nichte	niece
Die Eltern	parents

Die Schwester	sister	einzig	single
Der Sohn	son	dünn	skinny
Der Onkel	uncle	schlank	slim
Aussehen und Qualitäten	**Appearance and qualities**	gerade	straight
		stark	strong
aktiv	active	blöd	stupid
kahl	bald	taktvoll	tactful
Der Charakter	character	talentiert	talented
klug	clever	hoch	tall
rücksichtsvoll	considerate	dünn	thin
kreativ	creative	hässlich	ugly
grausam	cruel	unfreundlich	unkind
lockig	curly	schwach	weak
energetisch	energetic	jung	young
fett	fat	**Emotionen**	**Emotions**
großzügig	generous	gelangweilt	bored
gierig	greedy	zuversichtlich	confident
behaart	hairy	zufrieden	content
gut aussehend	handsome	neugierig	curious
freundlich	kind	begeistert	ecstatic
verheiratet	married	Die Emotion	emotion
alt	old	aufgeregt	excited
rundlich	plump	doof	goofy
höflich	polite	glücklich	happy
arm	poor	hoffend	hoping
ziemlich	pretty	hungrig	hungry
reich	rich	einsam	lonely
unhöflich	rude	spitzbübisch	mischievous
kurz	short	nervös	nervous

beleidigt	offended	Der Pyjama	pyjamas
traurig	sad	Die Regenjacke	raincoat
erschrocken	scared	Der Ring	ring
schockiert	shocked	Die Sandalen	sandals
schläfrig	sleepy	Der Schal	scarf
überrascht	surprised	Das Hemd	shirt
durstig	thirsty	Die Schuhe	shoes
müde	tired	Die kurze Hose	shorts
Kleider	**Clothes**	Der Rock	skirt
Der Anorak	anorak	Die Hausschuhe	slippers
Der Gürtel	belt	Die Turnschuhe	sneakers
Die Bluse	blouse	Die Socken	socks
Der Stiefel	boots	Die Strümpfe	stockings
Das Armband	bracelet	Der Anzug	suit
Die Kappe	cap	Das Sweatshirt	sweater
Die Strickjacke	cardigan	Der Badeanzug	swimsuit
Die Kleider	clothes	Die Krawatte	tie
Der Mantel	coat	Die Strumpfhose	tights
Das Kleid	dress	Der Trainingsanzug	tracksuit
Der Ohrring	earring	Die Hose	trousers
Der Pelzmantel	fur coat	Das T-Shirt	T-shirt
Die Brille	glasses	Der Regenschirm	umbrella
Der Handschuh	glove	Die Hose	pants
Der Hut	hat	Die Uhr	watch
Die Jacke	jacket	**Haus und Möbel**	**House and furniture**
Die Jeans	jeans	Der Wecker	alarm clock
Das Trikot	jersey	Die Wohnung	apartment
Die Halskette	necklace	Der Balkon	balcony
Das Nachthemd	nightie		

Das Badezimmer	bathroom
Das Bett	bed
Das Schlafzimmer	bedroom
Die Tagesdecke	bedspread
Die Bank	bench
Die Decke	blanket
Das Bücherregal	bookcase
Der Teppich	carpet
Die Schatulle	casket
Der Sessel	chair
Der Wandschrank	closet
Der Schrank	cupboard
Der Vorhang	curtain
Der Schreibtisch	desk
Das Esszimmer	dining room
Die Tür	door
Die Türklingel	doorbell
unten	downstairs
Die Möbel	furniture
Die Garage	garage
Der Flur	hall
Der Korridor	hallway
Das Haus	house
Das Innere	interior
Die Küche	kitchen
Die Lampe	lamp
Das Wohnzimmer	living room
Der Briefkasten	mailbox
Die Matratze	mattress
Der Spiegel	mirror
Der Nachttisch	nightstand
Das Bild	picture
Das Kissen	pillow
Der Kissenbezug	pillowcase
Das Dach	roof
Das Zimmer	room
Der Safe	safe
Das Blatt	sheet
Das Regal	shelf
Die Dusche	shower
Das Sofa	sofa
Die Treppe	stairs
Der Schemel	stool
Die Tabelle	table
Die Toilette	toilet
nach oben	upstairs
Das Fenster	window
Die Küche	**Kitchen**
Der Brenner	burner
Der Küchenschrank	cabinet
Der Kanister	canister
Der Sessel	chair
Das Kochbuch	cookbook
Der Geschirrspüler	dishwasher
Der Wasserhahn	faucet
Der Gefrierschrank	freezer
Die Küche	kitchen
Das Geschirr	kitchenware

Die Mikrowelle	microwave	Die Zuckerschüssel	sugar bowl
Der Ofen	oven	Das Geschirr	tableware
Der Kühlschrank	refrigerator	Die Teekanne	teapot
Das Waschbecken	sink	**Essen**	**Food**
Der Schwamm	sponge	gebacken	baked
Der Herd	stove	Die Bohne	bean
Die Tabelle	table	Das Rindfleisch	beef
Der Toaster	toaster	bitter	bitter
Das Handtuch	towel	Das Brot	bread
Das Geschirr	**Tableware**	Die Butter	butter
Die Flasche	bottle	Der Kuchen	cake
Die Schüssel	bowl	Die Süßigkeiten	candy
Die Kaffeetasse	coffeepot	Der Kaviar	caviar
Die Tasse	cup	Der Käse	cheese
Die Gabel	fork	Das Hähnchen	chicken
Die Bratpfanne	frying pan	Die Schokolade	chocolate
Das Glas	glass	Der Cocktail	cocktail
Der Krug	jug	Der Kakao	cocoa
Der Kessel	kettle	Der Kaffee	coffee
Das Messer	knife	Das Plätzchen	cookie
Der Deckel	lid	Das Croissant	croissant
Der Becher	mug	Das Kotelett	cutlet
Die Serviette	napkin	Das Ei	egg
Die Pfanne	pan	Der Fisch	fish
Der Pfefferstreuer	pepper shaker	Das Mehl	flour
Der Teller	plate	Das Lebensmittel	food
Der Salzstreuer	salt shaker	gebraten	fried
Der Kochtopf	saucepan	Die Frucht	fruit
Der Löffel	spoon	Der Schinken	ham

Das Eis	ice cream	süß	sweet
Die Marmelade	jam	Der Tee	tea
Das Gelee	jelly	Das Gemüse	vegetables
Der Saft	juice	**Fleisch und Fisch**	**Meat and fish**
Der Ketchup	ketchup	Das Fleisch	meat
Die Makkaroni	macaroni	Das Rindfleisch	beef
Die Mayonnaise	mayonnaise	Das Lamm	lamb
Das Fleisch	meat	Das Hammelfleisch	mutton
Die Milch	milk	Das Schweinefleisch	pork
Der Pfannkuchen	pancake	Das Kalbfleisch	veal
Die Pasta	pasta	Das Wild	venison
Der Pfeffer	pepper	Der Speck	bacon
Der Kuchen	pie	Der Schinken	ham
Die Pizza	pizza	Die Leber	liver
Das Schweinefleisch	pork	Die Nieren	kidneys
Der Haferbrei	porridge	Das Geflügel	poultry
Die Kartoffel	potato	Das Hähnchen	chicken
Der Reis	rice	Der Truthahn	turkey
Der Salat	salad	Die Ente	duck
Das Salz	salt	Die Gans	goose
gesalzen	salted	Der Fisch	fish
Das Sandwich	sandwich	Der Kabeljau	cod
Die Soße	sauce	Die Forelle	trout
Die Wurst	sausage	Der Lachs	salmon
Die Suppe	soup	Der Seehecht	hake
sauer	sour	Die Scholle	plaice
würzen	spice	Die Makrele	mackerel
Das Steak	steak	Die Sardine	sardine
Der Zucker	sugar	Der Hering	herring

Die Meeresfrüchte	seafood	Der Sellerie	celery
Die Garnele	prawn	Die Gurke	cucumber
Die Garnele	shrimp	Der Dill	dill
Die Muschel	mussel	Die Aubergine	eggplant
Die Auster	oyster	Der Knoblauch	garlic
Der Hummer	lobster	Die Zwiebel	onion
Der Tintenfisch	squid	Die Petersilie	parsley
Die Krabbe	crab	Die Erbse	pea
Die Frucht	**Fruit**	Der Pfeffer	pepper
Der Apfel	apple	Die Kartoffel	potato
Die Aprikose	apricot	Der Kürbis	pumpkin
Die Banane	banana	Der Rettich	radish
Die Frucht	fruit	Die Tomate	tomato
Die Traube	grape	Das Gemüse	vegetable
Die Grapefruit	grapefruit	**Die Getränke**	**Beverages**
Die Kiwi	kiwi	Alkohol	alcohol
Die Zitrone	lemon	alkoholisches Getränk	alcoholic beverage
Die Limette	lime	Das Bier	beer
Die Mango	mango	Das Getränk	beverage
Die Melone	melon	Der Cocktail	cocktail
Der Pfirsich	peach	Der Kakao	cocoa
Die Birne	pear	Der Kaffee	coffee
Die Ananas	pineapple	Das Getränk	drink
Die Pflaume	plum	Der Fruchtsaft	fruit juice
Das Gemüse	**Vegetables**	Der Eistee	iced tea
Die Bohnen	beans	Der Saft	juice
Die Zuckerrüben	beet	Die Limonade	lemonade
Der Kohl	cabbage	Die Milch	milk
Die Karotte	carrot	Der Milchshake	milkshake

Der Orangensaft	orange juice	waschen	wash
Das alkoholfreie Getränk	soft drink	wiegen	weigh
		verquirlen	whisk
Der Tee	tea	**Der Haushalt**	**Housekeeping**
Der Tomatensaft	tomato juice	Die Luft	air
Der Gemüsesaft	vegetable juice	bleichen	bleach
Das Wasser	water	Der Besen	broom
Der Wein	wine	Der Eimer	bucket
Das Kochen	**Cooking**	Das Reinigungsmittel	cleanser
hinzufügen	add	Die Wäscheklammer	clothespin
backen	bake	Der Schmutz	dirt
schlagen	beat	Der Staub	dust
kochen	boil	Die Schaufel	dustpan
hacken	chop	leer	empty
kochen	cook	Der Müll	garbage
kochend	cooking	Die Haushaltung	housekeeping
braten	fry	Das Bügeleisen	iron
reiben	grate	Das Bügelbrett	ironing board
grillen	grill	Die Wäsche	laundry
schmelzen	melt	Das Waschmittel	laundry detergent
zerkleinern	mince	Der Mopp	mop
mischen	mix	Der Lappen	rag
schälen	peel	Der Schwamm	sponge
gießen	pour	fegen	sweep
braten	roast	Der Mülleimer	trash can
sieben	sift	Der Staubsauger	vacuum cleaner
kochen	simmer	wischen	wipe
schneiden	slice	**Die Körperpflege**	**Body care**
rühren	stir	Die Pflege	care

Das Eau de Cologne	cologne	**Das Wetter**	**Weather**
Der Kamm	comb	Die Brise	breeze
Die Zahnseide	dental floss	hell	bright
Das Deodorant	deodorant	frostig	chilly
Der Ventilator	fan	bewölkt	cloudy
Das Erfrischungsmittel	freshener	kalt	cold
Die Haarnadel	hairpin	kühl	cool
Der Korb	hamper	Der Nebel	fog
Die Hygiene	hygiene	neblig	foggy
Der Lippenstift	lipstick	eisig	frosty
Die Wimperntusche	mascara	Der Hagel	hail
Der Spiegel	mirror	Die Hitze	heat
Das Mundwasser	mouthwash	heiß	hot
Die Nagelpolitur	nail polish	Der Blitz	lightning
Das Parfüm	perfume	Der Nebel	mist
Der Rasierer	razor	Der Regen	rain
Die Waage	scale	regnerisch	rainy
Die Schere	scissors	Der Regenschauer	shower
Das Shampoo	shampoo	Der Schnee	snow
Der Rasierschaum	shaving cream	sonnig	sunny
Die Dusche	shower	Die Temperatur	temperature
Das Waschbecken	sink	Das Wetter	weather
Die Seife	soap	Der Wind	wind
Der Schwamm	sponge	windig	windy
Die Toilette	toilet	**Der Transport**	**Transport**
Die Zahnbürste	toothbrush	Das Flugzeug	airplane
Die Zahnpasta	toothpaste	Der Krankenwagen	ambulance
Das Handtuch	towel	Das Fahrrad	bicycle
Die Pinzette	tweezers	Das Boot	boat

Der Bus	bus	Das Café	cafe
Das Auto	car	Der Parkplatz	car park
Der Hubschrauber	helicopter	Die Kirche	church
Das Motorrad	motorcycle	Das Kino	cinema
Das Polizeiauto	police car	Der Zirkus	circus
Die Straße	road	Die Stadt	city
Das Segelboot	sailboat	Das Café	coffee shop
Der Roller	scooter	Die Ecke	corner
Das Schiff	ship	Die Kreuzung	crossing
Die Straße	street	Die Fußgängerbrücke	crosswalk
Die Ampel	traffic light	Die Zahnarztpraxis	dentist's
Der Zug	train	Das Kaufhaus	department store
Die Tram	tram	Der Arzt	doctor's
Der Transport	transport	Die Drogerie	drugstore
Der LKW	truck	Die Feuerwehr	fire station
Der Van	van	Das Blumengeschäft	flower shop
Die Stadt	**City**	Das Blumenbeet	flower-bed
Die Gasse	alley	Der Brunnen	fountain
Der Bereich	area	Die Galerie	gallery
Die Allee	avenue	Die Tankstelle	gas station
Die Bäckerei	bakery	Das Tor	gate
Die Bank	bank	Der Friseur	hair salon
Die Bar	bar	Das Krankenhaus	hospital
Die Badeanstalt	baths	Das Hotel	hotel
Die Bank	bench	Die Straßenkreuzung	intersection
Die Buchhandlung	bookstore	Die Bibliothek	library
Die Brücke	bridge	Die Karte	map
Das Gebäude	building	Der Markt	market
Die Bushaltestelle	bus stop	Das Monument	monument

Das Kino	movie theater	Die U-Bahn	subway
Das Museum	museum	Der Supermarkt	supermarket
Der Nachtclub	nightclub	Das Schwimmbad	swimming pool
Der Palast	palace	Der Taxistand	taxi-rank
Der Park	park	Das Theater	theatre
Der Parkplatz	parking lot	Die Stadt	town
Das Pflaster	pavement	Der Stadtplan	town plan
Der Zebrastreifen	pedestrian crossing	Der Stadtplatz	town square
Die Apotheke	pharmacy	Die Ampeln	traffic lights
Die Bildergalerie	picture gallery	Der Bahnhof	train station
Die Polizei	police	Die Untergrundbahn	underground
Das Schwimmbad	pool	Die Unterführung	underpass
Die Post	post office	Die Universität	university
Das Restaurant	restaurant	Der Zoo	zoo
Die Straße	road	**Die Schule**	**School**
Das Straßenschild	road sign	Der Rucksack	backpack
Die Schule	school	Die Glocke	bell
Der Sitz	seat	Die Biologie	biology
Das Geschäft	shop	Die Tafel	blackboard
Der Bürgersteig	sidewalk	Die Unterbrechung	break
Der Wolkenkratzer	skyscraper	Der Taschenrechner	calculator
Der Platz	square	Der Sessel	chair
Das Stadion	stadium	Die Kreide	chalk
Der Stall	stall	Die Chemie	chemistry
Die Statue	statue	Die Klemme	clamp
Das Geschäft	store	Das Klassenzimmer	classroom
Die Straße	street	Der Clip	clip
Die Straßenkarte	street map	Das Klemmbrett	clipboard
Der Vorort	suburb	Die Uhr	clock

Die Korrekturflüssigkeit	correction fluid
Der Lehrplan	curriculum
Der Schreibtisch	desk
Die Zeichnung	drawing
Die Bildung	education
Der Radiergummi	eraser
Die Prüfung	exam
Die Untersuchung	examination
Die Datei	file
Die Erdkunde	geography
Der Globus	globe
kleben	glue
Der Schulleiter	headmaster
Der Textmarker	highlighter
Die Geschichte	history
Der Urlaub	holiday
Die Lektion	lesson
Das Schließfach	locker
Die Karte	map
Das Kennzeichen	mark
Der Marker	marker
Die Mathematik	mathematics
Die Musik	music
Das Notizbuch	notebook
Der Notizblock	notepad
Der Bürobedarf	office supplies
Das Papier	paper
Der Stift	pen
Der Bleistift	pencil
Das Mäppchen	pencil case
Die Physik	physics
der Locher	puncher
Der Schüler	pupil
Die Reißzwecke	pushpin
Das Lineal	ruler
Die Schule	school
Die Schere	scissors
Der Tesafilm	scotch tape
Das Semester	semester
Der Anspitzer	sharpener
Der Hefter	stapler
Die Heftklammern	staples
Die Schreibwaren	stationery
Der Aufkleber	sticker
Der Schüler	student
Das Band	tape
Der Lehrer	teacher
Der Test	test
Das Lehrbuch	textbook
Der Zeitplan	timetable
Die Berufe	**Professions**
Der Buchhalter	accountant
Der Schauspieler	actor
Der Administrator	administrator
Der Architekt	architect
Der Künstler	artist
Der Athlet	athlete

Der Herrenfriseur	barber	Der Musiker	musician
Der Barkeeper	barman	Die Krankenschwester	nurse
Der Leibwächter	bodyguard	Der Fotograf	photographer
Der Erbauer	builder	Der Klempner	plumber
Der Kassierer	cashier	Der Polizist	policeman
Der Reiniger	cleaner	Der Politiker	politician
Der Trainer	coach	Der Briefträger	postman
Der Komponist	composer	Der Priester	priest
Der Berater	consultant	Der Beruf	profession
Der Koch	cook	Der Programmierer	programmer
Der Kurier	courier	Der Wissenschaftler	scientist
Der Zahnarzt	dentist	Die Sekretärin	secretary
Der Designer	designer	Der Verkäufer	shop assistant
Der Arzt	doctor	Der Sänger	singer
Der Fahrer	driver	Der Stylist	stylist
Der Ökonom	economist	Der Taxifahrer	taxi driver
Der Elektriker	electrician	Der Lehrer	teacher
Der Ingenieur	engineer	Der Tierarzt	vet
Der Financier	financier	Die Bedienung	waiter
Der FeuerwehrmannDer	fireman	Der Schriftsteller	writer
Der Führer	guide	**Die Aktionen**	**Actions**
Der Friseur	hairdresser	biegen	bend
Der Dolmetscher	interpreter	tragen	carry
Der Journalist	journalist	fangen	catch
Der Anwalt	lawyer	kriechen	crawl
Der Bibliothekar	librarian	tauchen	dive
Manager	manager	ziehen	drag
Der Soldat	military (man)	schlagen	hit
		halten	hold

hüpfen	hop	Das Fagott	bassoon
springen	jump	Der Taktstock	baton
treten	kick	Der Bogen	bow
lehnen	lean	Die Blechbläser	brass instruments
aufheben	lift	Das Cello	cello
marschieren	march	Die Kammermusik	chamber music
ziehen	pull	Die Klarinette	clarinet
drücken	push	Die klassische Musik	classical music
stellen	put	komponieren	compose
laufen	run	Der Komponist	composer
sitzen	sit	Das Konzert	concert
überspringen	skip	Der Dirigent	conductor
schlagen	slap	Das Becken	cymbals
hocken	squat	Die Trommel	drum
strecken	stretch	Die Trommelstöcke	drum sticks
werfen	throw	Die Flöte	flute
auf Zehenspitzen gehen	tiptoe	Der Konzertflügel	grand piano
		Die Gitarre	guitar
gehen	walk	Die Harfe	harp
Die Musik	**Music**	Das Horn	horn
Die musikalische Begleitung	accompaniment	Die Instrumentalmusik	instrumental music
		Der Lautsprecher	loudspeaker
Das Akkordeon	accordion	Das Mikrofon	microphone
Das Album	album	Die Musikinstrumente	musical instruments
Der Dudelsack	bagpipe		
Die Balalaika	balalaika	Der Musiker	musician
Das Ballett	ballet	Die Oboe	oboe
Das Band	band	Die Oper	opera
Der Bass	bass	Die Operette	operetta

154

Das Orchester	orchestra	Das Radfahren	cycling
Die Orgel	organ	Das Tanzen	dancing
Das Schlagzeug	percussion	Das Tauchen	diving
Das Klavier	piano	Das Fußballspiel	football
Die Aufführung	recital	Das Golf	golf
Das Saxophon	saxophone	Die Gymnastik	gymnastics
Die Single	single	Das Eishockey	hockey
Der Solist	soloist	Das Jogging	jogging
Das Lied	song	Das Judo	judo
Der Klang	sound	Das Karate	karate
Die Streichinstrumente	string instruments	Das Fallschirmspringen	parachuting
Die Symphonie	symphony		
Der Synthesizer	synthesizer	Das Tischtennis	ping-pong
transkribieren	transcribe	Das Rennen	racing
Die Posaune	trombone	Das Segeln	sailing
Die Trompete	trumpet	Das Schießen	shooting
Die Tuba	tuba	Das Skateboarding	skateboarding
Das Video (Clip)	video (clip)	Das Skaten	skating
Die Viola	viola	Das Skifahren	skiing
Die Geige	violin	Das Schlittenfahren	sledding
Der Virtuose	virtuoso	Das Schwimmen	swimming
Die Blasinstrumente	wind instruments	Das Fußballspiel	soccer
Der Sport	**Sports**	Das Tennis	tennis
Das Aerobic	aerobics	Das Volleyballspiel	volleyball
die Leichtathletik	athletics	Das Gewichtheben	weightlifting
Das Basketballspiel	basketball	Das Ringen	wrestling
Das Bowling	bowling	Das Segeln	yachting
Das Boxen	boxing	**Der Körper**	**Body**
Der Kanusport	canoeing	Der Knöchel	ankle

Der Arm	arm
Der Rücken	back
kahl	bald
Der Bart	beard
Der Körper	body
Das Gesäß	bottom
Die Waden	calf (calves)
Die Wange	cheek
Die Brust	chest
Das Kinn	chin
Der Ellbogen	elbow
Das Auge (die Augen)	eye(s)
Die Augenbraue	eyebrow
Die Wimper	eyelash
Das Augenlid	eyelid
Das Gesicht	face
Der Finger	finger
Der Fingernagel	fingernail
Der Fuß (die Füße)	foot (feet)
Die Stirn	forehead
Die Brille	glasses
Das Haar	hair
behaart	hairy
Die Hand	hand
Der Kopf	head
Die Hacke	heel
Der Zeigefinger	index finger
Das Knie	knee
Das Bein	leg
Die Lippe(n)	lip(s)
Der kleine Finger	little finger
Der Mann	man
Der Mittelfinger	middle finger
Der Schnurrbart	moustache
Der Mund	mouth
Der Hals	neck
Die Nase	nose
Die Handinnenfläche	palm
Die Pupille	pupil
Der Ringfinger	ring finger
Das Schienbein	shin
Die Schulter	shoulder
Der Bauch	stomach
Die Sonnenbrille	sunglasses
Der Schenkel	thigh
Der Daumen	thumb
Die Zehe	toe
Der Zehennagel	toenail
Die Zunge	tongue
Der Zahn (die Zähne)	tooth (teeth)
Die Taille	waist
Die Frau	woman
Die Natur	**Nature**
Der Strand	beach
Die Schlucht	canyon
Die Küste	coast
Die Wüste	desert
Das Feld	field

Der Wald	forest	Die Fledermaus	bat
Der Gletscher	glacier	Der Bär	bear
Der Hügel	hill	Der Biber	beaver
Die Höhle	hollow	Der Bison	bison
Die Insel	island	Das Kamel	camel
Der Dschungel	jungle	Der Schimpanse	chimpanzee
Die See	lake	Der Hirsch	deer
Der Berg	mountain	Der Esel	donkey
Die Natur	nature	Der Elefant	elephant
Der Ozean	ocean	Der Fuchs	fox
Die Ebene	plain	Die Giraffe	giraffe
Der Teich	pond	Der Gorilla	gorilla
Der Fluss	river	Das Nilpferd	hippopotamus
Der Felsen	rock	Das Pferd	horse
Das Meer	sea	Die Hyäne	hyena
Das Haustier	**Pet**	Das Känguru	kangaroo
Die Katze	cat	Der Koala	koala
Der Hund	dog	Der Leopard	leopard
Das Meerschweinchen	guinea pig	Der Löwe	lion
Der Hamster	hamster	Das Lama	llama
Das Pferd	horse	Der Affe	monkey
Das Kätzchen	kitten	Der Elch	moose
Das Haustier	pet	Die Maus	mouse
Das Schwein	pig	Der Pandabär	panda
Das Ferkel	piglet	Das Schwein	pig
Der Welpe	puppy	Der Hase	rabbit
Der Hase	rabbit	Die Ratte	rat
Die Tiere	**Animals**	Das Nashorn	rhinoceros
Das Tier	animal	Der Skunk	skunk

Das Eichhörnchen	squirrel	Der Schwan	swan
Der Tiger	tiger	Der Specht	woodpecker
Der Wolf	wolf	**Die Blumen**	**Flowers**
Das Zebra	zebra	Der Strauß	bouquet
Die Vögel	**Birds**	Die Kamelie	camellia
Der Vogel	bird	Die Nelke	carnation
Der Kanarienvogel	canary	Der Krokus	crocus
Das Hühnchen	chicken	Die Narzisse	daffodil
Der Kranich	crane	Die Dahlie	dahlia
Die Krähe	crow	Das Gänseblümchen	daisy
Der Kuckuck	cuckoo	Der Löwenzahn	dandelion
Die Ente	duck	Die Blume	flower
Der Adler	eagle	Die Gladiole	gladiolus
Der Flamingo	flamingo	Die Iris	iris
Die Gans	goose	Das Lavendel	lavender
Der Falke	hawk	Die Lilie	lily
Der Kolibri	hummingbird	Der Lotus	lotus
Der Vogel Strauß	ostrich	Die Narzisse	narcissus
Die Eule	owl	Die Orchidee	orchid
Der Papagei	parrot	Die Pfingstrose	peony
Der Pfau	peacock	Der Mohn	poppy
Der Pelikan	pelican	Die Rose	rose
Der Pinguin	penguin	Das Schneeglöckchen	snowdrop
Der Fasan	pheasant	Die Sonnenblume	sunflower
Die Taube	pigeon	Die Tulpe	tulip
Die Möwe	seagull	Das Veilchen	violet
Der Spatz	sparrow	**Die Bäume**	**Trees**
Der Storch	stork	Die Akazie	bark
Die Schwalbe	swallow	Die Buche	beech

Die Birke	birch	Das Weichtier	mollusc
Der Ast	branch	Der Ozean	ocean
Die Kastanie	chestnut	Der Tintenfisch	octopus
Der Kegel	cone	Der Otter	otter
Die Tanne	fir	Das Meer	sea
Der Wald	forest	Die Seeschlange	sea snake
Das Blatt	leaf	Der Seehund	seal
Die Linde	linden	Der Hai	shark
Der Ahorn	maple	Die Meeresfrüchte	shellfish
Die Eiche	oak	Die Garnele	shrimp
Die Palme	palm	Die Schnecke	snail
Die Kiefer	pine	Der Seestern	starfish
Die Pappel	poplar	Der Schwertfisch	swordfish
Die Wurzel	root	Die Schildkröte	tortoise
Der Baum	tree	Die Schildkröte	turtle
Der Baumstamm	trunk	Das Walross	walrus
Die Weide	willow	Der Wal	whale
Das Meer	**Sea**	**Die Farben**	**Colors**
Der Alligator	alligator	gelb	Yellow
Der Cachalot	cachalot	grün	green
Die Koralle	coral	blau	blue
Die Krabbe	crab	braun	brown
Der Flusskrebs	crayfish	weiß	white
Das Krokodil	crocodile	rot	red
Der Delfin	dolphin	orange	orange
Der Fisch	fish	rosa	pink
Der Frosch	frog	grau	gray
Die Qualle	jellyfish	schwarz	black
Der Hummer	lobster		

Die Größe	**Size**
Die Größe	size
klein	small
groß	big
mittel	medium
klein	little
groß	large
enorm	huge
lang	long
kurz	short
breit	wide
eng	narrow
hoch	high
groß	tall
niedrig	low
tief	deep
flach	shallow
dick	thick
dünn	thin
weit	far
in der Nähe von	near

Die Materialien	**Materials**
Der Ziegel	brick
Der Karton	cardboard
Der Lehm	clay
Das Tuch	cloth
Der Beton	concrete
Das Glas	glass
Das Leder	leather
Das Material	material
Das Metall	metal
Das Papier	paper
Der Kunststoff	plastic
Das Gummi	rubber
Der Stein	stone
Das Holz	wood
Der Stoff	fabric

Der Flughafen	**Airport**
Das Flugzeug	(air)plane
Der Flughafen	airport
Der Gang	aisle
Die Armlehne	armrest
Der Rucksack	backpack
Das Gepäck	baggage
Das Einsteigen	boarding
Die Kabine	cabin
Das Fortfahren	carry-on
Der Cockpit	cockpit
Der Zoll	customs
Die Verzögerung	delay
Das Reiseziel	destination
Der Notfall	emergency
Der Flug	flight
Der Rumpf	fuselage
Das Gate	gate
Die Landung	landing
Die Toilette	lavatory
Die Rettungsweste	life vest

Die Flüssigkeit	liquid	Der Gletscher	glacier
Der Passagier	passenger	Der Hügel	hill
Der Reisepass	passport	Der Berg	mountain
Die Startbahn	runway	Die Bergkette / Bergkette -	mountain chain
Der Zeitplan	schedule		
Der Sitz	seat	Der Pass	pass
Der Sicherheitsbeamte	security, guard	Die Spitze	peak
Der Koffer	suitcase	Die Ebene	plain
Das Heck	tail	Das Plateau	plateau
Das Abheben	takeoff	Der Gipfel	summit
Der Terminal	terminal	Das Tal	valley
Die Fahrkarte	ticket	Der Vulkan	volcano
Der Wagen	trolley	Die Wüste	desert
Das Fahrwerk	undercarriage	Der Äquator	equator
Das Visum	visa	Der Wald	forest
Das Fenster	window	Das Hochland	highlands
Der Flügel	wing	Der Dschungel	jungle
Die Erdkunde	**Geography**	Das Tiefland	lowlands
Der Bereich	area	Die Oase	oasis
Die Hauptstadt	capital	Der Sumpf	swamp
Die Stadt	city	Die Tropen	tropics
Das Land	country	Die Tundra	tundra
Der Kreis	district	Der Kanal	canal
Die Region	region	Die See	lake
Das Bundesland	state	Der Ozean	ocean
Die Stadt	town	Die Meeresströmung	ocean current
Das Dorf	village	Der Pool / Teich	pool / pond
Das Kap	cape	Der Fluss	river
Das Kliff	cliff	Das Meer	sea

Die Quelle	spring	Das unerlaubte Betreten	trespassing
Der Strom	stream		
Das Verbrechen	**Crimes**	**Nummern**	**Numbers**
Die Brandstiftung	arson	eins	one
Der Angriff	assault	zwei	two
Die Bigamie	bigamy	drei	three
Die Erpressung	blackmail	vier	four
Die Bestechung	bribery	fünf	five
Der Einbruch	burglary	sechs	six
Der Kindesmissbrauch	child abuse	Sieben	seven
Die Verschwörung	conspiracy	acht	eight
Die Spionage	espionage	neun	nine
Die Fälschung	forgery	zehn	ten
Der Betrug	fraud	elf	eleven
Der Völkermord	genocide	zwölf	twelve
Die Entführung	hijacking	dreizehn	thirteen
Der Mord	homicide	vierzehn	fourteen
Die Entführung	kidnapping	fünfzehn	fifteen
Der Totschlag	manslaughter	sechzehn	sixteen
Der Überfall	mugging	siebzehn	seventeen
Der Mord	murder	achtzehn	eighteen
Der Meineid	perjury	neunzehn	nineteen
Die Vergewaltigung	rape	zwanzig	twenty
Das Randalieren	riot	einundzwanzig	twenty-one
Der Raub	robbery	zweiundzwanzig	twenty-two
Der Ladendiebstahl	shoplifting	dreißig	thirty
Die Verleumdung	slander	vierzig	forty
Der Schmuggel	smuggling	fünfzig	fifty
Der Verrat	treason	sechzig	sixty

siebzig	seventy
achtzig	eighty
neunzig	ninety
einhundert	one hundred
einhundertundeins …	one hundred and one …
zweihundert	two hundred
eintausend	one thousand
eine Million	one million

Ordnungszahlen — **Ordinal numbers**

erste	first
zweite	second
dritte	third
vierte	fourth
fünfte	fifth
sechste	sixth
siebte	seventh
achte	eighth
neunte	ninth
zehnte	tenth
elfte	eleventh
zwölfte	twelfth
dreizehnte	thirteenth
vierzehnte	fourteenth
fünfzehnte	fifteenth
sechzehnte	sixteenth
siebzehnte	seventeenth
achtzehnte	eighteenth
neunzehnte	nineteenth
zwanzigste	twentieth
einundzwanzigste	twenty-first
zweiundzwanzigste	twenty-second
dreiundzwanzigste	twenty-third
vierundzwanzigste	twenty-fourth
fünfundzwanzigste	twenty-fifth
sechsundzwanzigste	twenty-sixth
siebenundzwanzigste	twenty-seventh
achtundzwanzigste	twenty-eighth
neunundzwanzigste	twenty-ninth
dreißigste	thirtieth
vierzigste	fortieth
fünfzigste	fiftieth
sechzigste	sixtieth
siebzigste	seventieth
achtzigste	eightieth
neunzigste	ninetieth
hundertste	hundredth
tausendste	thousandth
millionste	millionth

Recommended reading

First German Reader for Beginners (Volume 1)
Bilingual for Speakers of English
Beginner Elementary (A1 A2)

The book consists of Elementary and Pre-intermediate courses with parallel German-English texts. The author maintains learners' motivation by funny stories about real life situations such as meeting people, studying, job searches, working etc. The ALARM Method (Approved Learning Automatic Remembering Method) utilize natural human ability to remember words used in texts repeatedly and systematically. The author had to compose each sentence using only words explained in previous chapters. The second and the following chapters of the Elementary course have only about thirty new words each. The audio tracks are available inclusive on www.lppbooks.com/German

First German Reader (Volume 2)
Bilingual for Speakers of English
Elementary (A2)

This book is Volume 2 of First German Reader for Beginners. There are simple and funny German texts for easy reading. The book consists of Elementary course with parallel German-English texts. The author maintains learners' motivation with funny stories about real life situations such as meeting people, studying, job searches, working etc. The ALARM method utilize natural human ability to remember words used in texts repeatedly and systematically. The audio tracks and samples are available inclusive on www.lppbooks.com/German

First German Reader (Volume 3)
Bilingual for Speakers of English
Elementary (A2)

This book is Volume 3 of First German Reader for Beginners. There are simple and funny German texts for easy reading. The book consists of Elementary course with parallel German-English texts. The author maintains learners' motivation with funny stories about real life situations such as meeting people, studying, job searches, working etc. The ALARM method utilize natural human ability to remember words used in texts repeatedly and systematically. The audio tracks and samples are available inclusive on www.lppbooks.com/German

Second German Reader
Bilingual for Speakers of English
Elementary Pre-Intermediate (A2 B1)

A private detective is following the girl he is in love with. A former air force pilot, he is discovering some sides in the human nature he can't deal with. This book makes use of the ALARM Method to efficiently teach its reader German words, sentences and dialogues. The audio tracks and samples are available inclusive on www.lppbooks.com/German

First German Reader for Beginners
Bilingual for Children and Parents
Beginner (A1)

The book contains a beginner's course for children with parallel German-English translation. There are a few pictures and the first simple sentences in the first chapter. More pictures and vocabulary are added in the second and following chapters. They build up little stories, guiding a learner gently into the English language. The method ALARM utilize natural human ability to remember words used in texts repeatedly and systematically. The audio tracks and samples are available inclusive on www.lppbooks.com/German

First German Reader for Students
Bilingual for Speakers of English
Beginner Elementary (A1 A2)

German language learners can learn vocabulary and grammar usage with First German Reader for Students easily and fast. Each chapter is filled with words that are organized by topic, then used in a story in German. Questions and answers rephrase information and text is repeated in English to aid comprehension. The quick and easy-to-use format organizes many of life's situations from knowing your way around the house, studying at university, or getting a job. First German Reader for Students makes use of the ALARM Method to efficiently teach its reader German words, sentences and dialogues. The audio tracks and samples are available inclusive on www.lppbooks.com/German

First German Reader for Cooking
Bilingual for Speakers of English
Beginner Elementary (A1 A2)

When learning a language, familiarity in the subject helps connect one language to another. The First German Reader for Cooking provides the words and phrases in both English and German. Twenty-five chapters are divided into themes and topics related to cooking and food. Recipe directions along with easy questions and answers demonstrate the usage of these words and phrases. Supplementary resources include the German/English and English/German dictionaries. It might make you hungry or it might help German language learners like you improve their understanding in a familiar setting of the kitchen. The audio tracks and samples are available inclusive on www.lppbooks.com/German

First German Reader for Business
Bilingual for Speakers of English
Beginner Elementary (A1 A2)

The German you learn in high school or college does not always include the vocabulary you need in a professional environment. The First German Reader for Business is a resource that guides conversational bilinguals with the German vocabulary, phrases, and questions that are relevant to many situations in the workplace. With 25 chapters on topics from the office to software and supplementary resources including the German/English and English/German dictionaries, it is the book to help the businessperson take their German language knowledge to the professional level. The audio tracks and samples are available inclusive on www.lppbooks.com/German

First German Medical Reader for Health Professions and Nursing
Bilingual for Speakers of English
Bilingual for Speakers of English
Beginner Elementary (A1 A2)

First German Medical Reader will give you the words and phrases necessary for helping patients making appointments, informing them of their diagnosis, and their treatment options. Medical specialties range from ENT to dentistry. The ALARM method utilize natural human ability to remember words used in texts repeatedly and systematically. The author composed each sentence using only words explained in previous chapters. Supplementary resources include the German/English and English/German dictionaries, audio tracks, the 1300 important German words. Use this book to take your German knowledge to the health professional's level. The audio tracks are available inclusive on www.lppbooks.com/German/FGMR/

First German Reader for the Family
Bilingual for Speakers of English
Beginner Elementary (A1 A2)

How do you ask in a clear and precise way about relatives of your friends? How do you answer questions about your family and other beloved ones? Ask and answer questions about situations at home, on your way to school or university, at work, in hospital etc. The book makes use of the ALARM Method to efficiently teach its reader German words, sentences and dialogues. Through this method, a person will be able to enhance his or her ability to remember the words that has been incorporated into consequent sentences. The audio tracks and samples are available inclusive on www.lppbooks.com/German

Thomas's Fears and Hopes
Short Stories in Plain Spoken German
Bilingual for speakers of English
Pre-intermediate Level

Thomas had returned home to Georgia for his father's funeral. He became informed that he would receive the entire estate as he was the only child. Then a few events happened that scared him. The audio tracks are available inclusive on www.lppbooks.com/German/SSPSG/

First German Reader for Tourists
Bilingual for Speakers of English
Beginner (A1)

If you would like to travel and learn German at A1 level, this book is the best choice. Unlike a phrasebook, it is composed with the thought of systematic learning approach. The book makes use of the ALARM Method to efficiently teach its reader German words, sentences and dialogues. Through this method, a person will be able to enhance his or her ability to remember the words that has been incorporated into consequent sentences. The audio tracks and samples are available inclusive on www.lppbooks.com/German

Learn German Language Through Dialogue
Bilingual for Speakers of English
Beginner Elementary (A1 A2)

The textbook gives you a lot of examples on how questions in German should be formed. It is easy to see the difference between German and English using parallel translation. Common questions and answers used in everyday situations are explained simply enough even for beginners. Some sayings and jokes make it engaging despite four cases that make German a little difficult for some students. The audio tracks and samples are available inclusive on www.lppbooks.com/German

Die Abenteuer von Benny & Ollie in gefährlichen Situationen

Tips for discussing child safety and what you can do to help your child. Tips for parents to help their children stay safe and what your child can do. Outside and at home. This bilingual book contains German-English parallel translation.

Fremde Wasser
Intermediate German Reader
Parallel translation for speakers of English

Being a co-founder of a two-men business has it's pros and cons. However the cold waters of self-employment do not fit everyone. The audio tracks are available inclusive on www.lppbooks.com/German/BSE

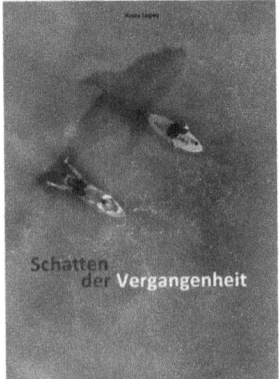

Schatten der Vergangenheit
Intermediate level
Bilingual for Speakers of English

Forensic science was one of Damien Morin's passions. However, the first real crime that he investigated led him to his own past. The audio tracks are available inclusive on www.audiolego.com/German/Lopez/En

Wer verlor das Geld? Who lost the money?
First German Reader for Beginner and Elementary Level
Bilingual with German-English Translation

The first part of the book explains with examples of basic sentence structure of German language. The German and English texts are located parallel for easier understanding. Each chapter contains patterns of basic sentence structure according to two or three grammar topics. The second part of the book, which is also composed of simple sentences, represents a detective story. The ALARM method utilize natural human ability to remember words used in texts repeatedly and systematically. The audio tracks are available inclusive on www.lppbooks.com/German/WLM/